155- 186

237- 256

Additional Praise for
The Little Book of Economics

"The data are well chosen and the writing is decidedly unwonky. Ip skillfully includes essential economic history without making readers feel as though a time warp has thrown them back into an unpleasant undergraduate economics course. . . . 'A must-read in economic literacy.'"

—*USA Today*

"If you've never read anything about economics but have often wondered about it, this is, quite simply, the best book for you to read. It's short, but packs in a lot of information without becoming boring and often with a small, healthy dose of humor. It's very, very readable and could be digested on an airplane flight. More importantly, it gives you just enough connections between events and economic theory to pull you deeper into topics that interest you and makes reading economic news that much easier."

—Trent Hamm,
The Christian Science Monitor online

THE LITTLE BOOK

OF
ECONOMICS

Little Book Big Profits Series

In the *Little Book Big Profits* series, the brightest icons in the financial world write on topics that range from tried-and-true investment strategies to tomorrow's new trends. Each book offers a unique perspective on investing, allowing the reader to pick and choose from the very best in investment advice today.

Books in the *Little Book Big Profits* series include:

THE LITTLE BOOK

OF
ECONOMICS

*How the Economy Works in the
Real World*

REVISED AND UPDATED

GREG IP

FOREWORD BY MOHAMED EL-ERIAN

WILEY

John Wiley & Sons, Inc.

Library of Congress Cataloging-in-Publication Data:

Ip, Greg, 1964-
 The little book of economics : how the economy works in the real world / Greg Ip; foreword by Mohamed A. El-Erian. — Rev. and updated.
 p. cm. — (Little book big profits series)
 ISBN 978-1-118-39157-0 (cloth); 978-1-118-42178-9 (ebk); 978-1-118-58217-6 (ebk); 978-1-118-41753-9 (ebk)
 1. Economics. 2. United States—Economic conditions. I. Title.
HB171.I69 2013
330—dc23
 2012044347

Printed in the United States of America
10 9 8 7 6 5 4 3 2

To Natalie and Daniel

Contents

—————— ≈ ——————

Foreword

It was as a 15-year-old at school in England that I was formally introduced to the subject of economics. And I immediately fell in love with it. Here was a subject that provided me with valuable tools to think about a range of everyday topics, to formulate answers from first principles, and to pose additional interesting questions whose answers I was also eager to know.

My love affair with economics has blossomed and continues today. And I feel privileged as economics seems to be even more relevant and topical as time passes. It facilitates our understanding of the well-being of societies, and the challenges they face; it explains many of the daily interactions between individuals, companies, and governments; and it offers a guide to understanding political and social trends that are shaping our world.

Simply put, economics is the key to understanding and analyzing both what is likely to happen and what should happen. Yet, as a topic, it is also horribly misunderstood and often overlooked.

Many believe that economics is too complex, too mathematical, and too arcane for them. Others question the benefits of investing their time and effort to get to know a subject that is the source of endless jokes, including presidential ones. (For example, President Harry S. Truman is said to have famously asked for a one-handed economist, noting that "all my economists say, on the one hand and on the other.")

Why am I telling you all this? Because I have come across a book that makes economics brilliantly accessible and, also, lots of fun. (Yes, economics can be fun!)

Forget about those heavy textbooks. Instead, read Greg Ip's book. It is well written and highly engaging. Moreover, it could not have been written by a more qualified person, and it could not come at a better time.

Greg first came to my attention, and that of my professional colleagues, through his reporting and analyses at the *Wall Street Journal*. We would all eagerly look forward to his columns for insights into economic developments and the outlook for policy.

Greg's work at the *Wall Street Journal*, and now the *Economist*, is based on careful, in-depth research. It uses

a robust set of analytical frameworks and reflects access to top policy makers and thinkers. And it is always relevant and timely. His columns have been the catalyst for interesting discussions at PIMCO's Investment Committee as we all tried to better understand developments and frame our shared outlook for the economy and markets.

In his elegant book, Greg takes us on an informative and stimulating economic journey. We make multiple stops as we get exposed to basic topics (such as the drivers of economic growth and welfare) and delicate balances (such as the tug of war between inflation and deflation). We learn about how government actions impact the economy—be it through the familiar channel of public finances and interest rates, or the more complex web of regulations and prudential supervision.

The book offers us a wonderful mix of perspectives. We are treated to broad overview analyses that are reminiscent of looking at the landscape from a plane flying at 30,000 feet in a cloudless sky. We are also exposed to careful micro discussions, finding ourselves, as Greg puts it, "inside the sausage factory."

As his loyal readers would expect—and there are many of them—Greg's book also includes delightful discussions of one of his favorite topics, namely, the design and operation of monetary policy. We get a rare

view into the mysterious world of the U.S. Federal Reserve where technocratic competence has to be combined with political savvy and judgment calls about the inherently uncertain balance of future risks and opportunities—be it in Europe, the United States, or the rest of the world.

The book also provides us with numerous examples of how all this analysis applies to companies and people that are familiar to most of us. Indeed, the frequent real-world snippets and text boxes are a great reminder of how economics plays out every day in the world around us.

Greg did more than produce an elegant book. He did so at a great time.

The global economy today is in a multiyear process of resetting after the 2008 to 2009 global financial crisis. This historical phenomenon is full of unfamiliar dynamics. It constantly questions "conventional wisdom," gives rise to what was previously deemed unthinkable, and proceeds in a highly uneven, bumpy, and often surprising fashion.

No wonder economics features so prominently on the front pages of daily newspapers around the world. In industrial countries, there are frequent reports on the unusual level and composition of unemployment, the explosion in public debt and deficits, the volatility of

exchange rates, the prospect for higher taxation, and the still fragile state of the banking system. Moreover, Europe is in the midst of what many regard as an "existential challenge." Meanwhile, in major emerging economies, you will find a growing number of people questioning the sustainability of the development breakout phases, analyzing how best to control inflation and asset bubbles, how to immunize their economies against the headwinds from the industrial countries, and how also to counter protectionist pressures from abroad.

Greg assembles and analyzes these pressing themes in a work that is as much a guidebook for our times as an explainer of economics. His brilliant book helps you identify and understand the economic forces that are dramatically reshaping the globe today, and having a major impact on our social and political outlook. It exposes you to the key issues in an engaging and enjoyable fashion. Even seemingly old hands like me end up learning and relearning critical aspects of this fascinating and relevant topic.

I hope that you enjoy this book as much as I did. It's a must-read for all those wishing to understand what today's world holds in store for them, for their children, and for their grandchildren.

—Mohamed A. El-Erian

Introduction

~

FOR MOST AMERICANS, THE economy is like the plumbing: something to ignore as long as it's working. In the past five years, it feels like every pipe in the house has burst. Americans have endured a financial crisis, the worst recession and weakest recovery in memory, exploding government debt, and the threatened breakup of Europe's single currency.

In the presidential elections of both 2008 and 2012, the economy trumped all other issues by a gaping margin. Economists have been repeatedly surprised by events, and often can't agree on what to do about them. Yet people are hungrier than ever for their insight, devouring economics-themed blogs and hundreds of new books about the economy. "Like being an undertaker

during a plague, business is good for the economics profession," Greg Mankiw, an economics professor at Harvard University, wrote on his blog.

I have been following the economy since—well, childhood. My mother was an economist (long since retired) who delighted in applying the dismal science to raising her four children. I'm sure we were the only kids in town whose weekly allowance was indexed to inflation. I took economics in college, though not intending to write about it; I just wanted a fallback in case journalism didn't work out. Right out of college, I joined a metropolitan daily newspaper that put me on the night shift covering local politics, crime, and the like, a lot of which never made it into the paper. The business section, however, had lots of space in it and regular hours, so I got a transfer. Soon, I was writing about the economy and the markets, and loving it.

After years of interviewing policy makers, investors, and business leaders, I have found that the economy in the real world often differs from the economy in textbooks. Simple concepts like growth, unemployment, and government debt can be measured in multiple ways. Central banks don't think about inflation the way textbooks do. And the subject is often cloaked in dry numbers and mystifying language.

I wrote *The Little Book of Economics* to provide non-economists with a practical, plain-language guide to the concepts they encounter in their daily lives, whether as students, business managers, or concerned citizens, from growth, unemployment, and inflation to deficits, globalization, and the Federal Reserve. But the world keeps changing and in the past two years, new forces and insights have emerged. Let me note three in particular.

First, I've discovered my economics textbooks still have plenty to offer. Take interest rates. You can think of them as a price that must rise or fall so that the supply and demand for saving are in balance. For most of my career, policy makers tended to worry about too much borrowing and rising inflation and investors fretted about interest rates heading up.

The past few years are a reminder that the opposite can also happen. If everyone wants to save and no one wants (or is able) to borrow, interest rates can fall to zero and remain there, and spending will remain moribund. Government deficits may be essential—because if no one else is borrowing, someone has to. The economic concepts behind these phenomena were first developed in the 1930s, and as Paul Krugman, a Nobel Prize–winning economist, notes, many economists have

since forgotten them. That included me. I have since rediscovered them in my old textbooks.

Second, seemingly sensible economic solutions often fail the test of political acceptability. Recovering from a financial crisis can be hastened if the government buys up private borrowers' bad debts and makes them less onerous. But voters don't want their taxes subsidizing bankers or spendthrifts. Deep divisions among American politicians on how to solve its fiscal problems have made it difficult to put forward solutions that even economists agree would be helpful, such as a higher gasoline tax or a later retirement age.

Third, the rest of the world's influence on the economic lives of Americans has grown dramatically. Global markets determine the price of oil, gold, and increasingly interest rates, and even wages. Understanding where the American economy is going depends increasingly on decisions in Frankfurt and Beijing, not just New York and Washington.

This edition of *The Little Book of Economics* has been extensively revised and updated to reflect all these things, and more. A new chapter on currencies explains the euro crisis. As in the original, I've used simple language, examples, analogies, and minimal numbers, without sacrificing the underlying theory. While I've avoided jargon, the rest of the world isn't so considerate, and so

each chapter has a section called "Into the Weeds," which explains the essential data, people, and lingo of each subject. They're perfect primers for anyone who wants to follow the markets and the economy in detail. I've boiled down everything in each chapter to "The Bottom Line." If you read nothing else in the chapter, read this: It will tell you the essentials in a few short sentences. Finally, those who want to dive deeper can visit my website, www.gregip.com, where I have a section suggesting books, articles, and resources on the topics covered here along with my latest articles.

We've been through a lot of trauma in the past few years, but economics still provides essential tools for understanding what is going on. This book puts those tools in your hands.

Chapter One

The Secrets
of Success

*How People, Capital, and Ideas
Make Countries Rich*

Pop quiz: The year is 1990. Which of the following countries has the brighter future?

The first country leads all major economies in growth. Its companies have taken commanding market shares in electronics, cars, and steel, and are set to dominate banking. Its government and business leaders are

paragons of long-term strategic thinking. Budget and trade surpluses have left the country rich with cash.

The second country is on the brink of recession; its companies are deeply in debt or being acquired. Its managers are obsessed with short-term profits while its politicians seem incapable of mustering a coherent industrial strategy.

You've probably figured out that the first country is Japan and the second is the United States. And if the evidence persuaded you to put your money on Japan, you would have been in great company. "Japan has created a kind of automatic wealth machine, perhaps the first since King Midas," Clyde Prestowitz, a prominent pundit, wrote in 1989, while the United States was a "colony-in-the-making." Kenneth Courtis, one of the foremost experts on Japan's economy, predicted that in a decade's time it would approach the U.S. economy's size in dollar terms. Investors were just as bullish; at the start of the decade Japan's stock market was worth 50 percent more than that of the United States.

Persuasive though it was, the bullish case for Japan turned out completely wrong. The next decade turned expectations upside down. Japan's economic growth screeched to a halt, averaging just 1 percent from 1991 to 2000. Meanwhile, the United States shook off its

early 1990s lethargy and its economy was booming by the decade's end. In 2000, Japan's economy was only half as big as the U.S. economy. The Nikkei finished down 50 percent, while U.S. stocks rose more than 300 percent. Far from catching up to the United States, Japan's economy in 2010 fell to third largest in the world, behind China's.

What explains Japan's reversal of fortune? Simply put, an economy needs both healthy *demand* and *supply*. As is well known, Japan's *demand* for goods and services suffered when overinflated stocks and real estate collapsed, saddling companies and banks with bad debts that they had to work off. At the same time, though less well known, deep-seated forces chipped away at Japan's ability to *supply* goods and services.

The supply problem is critical because in the long run economic growth hinges on a country's productive potential, which in turn rests on three things:

1. Population
2. Capital (i.e., investment)
3. Ideas

Population is the source of future workers. Because of a low birth rate, an aging population and virtually

nonexistent immigration, Japan's working-age population began shrinking in the 1990s. A smaller workforce limits how much an economy can produce.

Capital and ideas are essential for making those workers productive. In the decades after World War II, Japan invested heavily in its human and economic capital. It educated its people and equipped them with cutting-edge technology adapted from the most advanced Western economies in an effort to catch up. By the 1990s, though, it had largely caught up. Once it had reached the frontier of technology, pushing that frontier outward would mean letting old industries die so that capital and workers could move to new ones. Japan's leaders resisted the bankruptcies and layoffs necessary for that to happen. As a result, the next wave of technological progress, based on the Internet, took root in the United States, whose economic lead over Japan grew sharply over the course of the 1990s.

A Recipe for Economic Growth

Numerous factors determine a country's success and whether its companies are good investments. Inflation and interest rates, consumer spending, and business confidence are important in the short run. In the long run, though, a country becomes rich or stagnates depending on whether it has the right mix of people,

capital, and ideas. Get these fundamentals right, and the short-run gyrations seldom matter.

~

Until the eighteenth century, economic growth was so slight it was almost impossible to distinguish the average Englishman's standard of living from his parents'.

Between 1945 and 2007 the U.S. economy went through 10 recessions yet still grew enough to end up six times larger, with the average American three times richer.

We've taken growth for granted for so long that we've forgotten that stagnation could ever be the norm. Yet, it once was. Until the eighteenth century, economic growth was so slight it was almost impossible to distinguish the average Englishman's standard of living from his parents.' Starting in the eighteenth century, this changed. The Industrial Revolution brought about a massive reorganization of production in England in the mid-1700s and later in Western Europe and North America. Since then, steady growth—the kind that the average person notices—has been the norm. According

to economic historian Angus Maddison, the average European was four times richer in 1952 than in 1820 and the average American was eight times richer.

In the preindustrial era, China was the world's largest economy. Its modest standard of living was on a par with that of Europe and the United States. But China then stagnated under the pressure of rebellion, invasion, and a hidebound bureaucracy that was hostile to private enterprise. The average Chinese was poorer in 1952 than in 1820.

So why do some countries grow and some stagnate? In a nutshell, growth rests on two building blocks: population and productivity.

1. *Population* determines how many workers a country will have.
2. *Productivity*, or output per worker, determines how much each worker earns.

The total output a country can produce given its labor force and its productivity is called *potential output*, and the rate at which that capacity grows over time is *potential growth*. So if the labor force grows 1 percent a year and its productivity by 1.5 percent, then potential growth is 2.5 percent. Thus, an economy grows.

Take a Growing Population

Let's recap. An economy needs workers to grow. And, usually, the higher the population, the higher the number of potential workers. Population growth depends on a number of factors including the number of women of child-bearing age, the number of babies each of those women has (the fertility rate), how long people live, and migration.

In poor countries, many children die young so mothers have more babies. As countries get richer and fewer children die, fertility rates drop and, eventually, so does population growth. As women have fewer children, more of them go to work. This *demographic dividend* delivers a one-time kick to economic growth. For example, it was a major contributor to East Asia's growth from the 1960s onward and to China's after the introduction of its one-child policy in 1979. But a country only gets to cash in its demographic dividend once. Eventually, as population growth slows, it ages and each worker must support a growing number of retirees. If fertility drops much below 2.1 babies per woman, the population will shrink unless offset by immigration.

Japan is not the only country to have experienced this; 40 percent of countries now have fertility rates

below 2.1, including Korea and Brazil. In some, including Russia and Germany, population is already shrinking. The most dramatic example is China where the one-child policy and, more recently, increasing wealth and urbanization have brought the fertility rate down dramatically to just 1.6. In Shanghai, China's wealthiest big city, it's 0.6, one of the lowest in the world. In 2026, China's population should start to decline. It may be the first country to grow old before it grows rich.

Add Capital

A country is not rich, though, just because it has a lot of people—just look at the Philippines, which has 21 times as many people as Ireland but an economy of roughly equal size.

The reason for this population/economic size disparity is that the average Filipino is much less productive than the average Irishman. For a country to be rich—that is, for its average citizen to enjoy a high standard of living—it must depend on productivity, which is the ability to make more, better stuff with the labor it already has.

Productivity itself depends on two factors: capital and ideas.

You can raise productivity by equipping workers with more capital, which means investing in land,

buildings, or equipment. Give a farmer more land and a bigger tractor or pave a highway to get his crops to market, and he'll grow more food at a lower cost. Capital is not free, though. A dollar invested to produce more stuff tomorrow is a dollar not available to spend on stuff today. Thus, for someone to invest a dollar, someone else must save a dollar; and so a key ingredient of growth is saving. That saving can come from households, businesses, foreigners, even governments, although most governments borrow rather than save, as we see in Chapter 14. The more a society saves, the more capital it can accumulate. (There is, however, such a thing as saving too much, as we learn in Chapter 11.)

Capital, though, will only take a country so far. Just as your second cup of coffee will perk you up less than your first, each additional dollar invested provides a smaller boost to production. A farmer's second tractor will help his productivity far less than his first. This is the *law of diminishing returns.*

Season with Ideas

How do you repeal the law of diminishing returns? With ideas. In 1989, Greg LeMond put bars on the front of his bicycle that enabled him to ride in a more aerodynamic position. This simple idea sliced seconds

off his time, allowing him to beat Laurent Fignon and win the Tour de France.

New ideas transform economic production the same way. By combining the capital and labor we already have differently, we can produce new or better products at a lower cost. "Economic growth springs from better recipes, not just from more cooking," says Paul Romer, a Stanford University economist. For example, DuPont's discovery of nylon in the 1930s transformed textile production. These man-made fibers could be spun at far higher speeds and required far fewer steps than cotton or wool. Combined with faster looms, textile productivity has soared, and clothes have gotten cheaper and better.

The productive power of ideas is nothing short of miraculous. Investing in more buildings and machines costs money. But a new idea can be reproduced endlessly for free.

The productive power of ideas is nothing short of miraculous. Investing in more buildings and machines costs money. But a new idea can be reproduced endlessly

for free. Just as other cyclists quickly copied Greg LeMond's aerobars, companies catch up to their competitors by copying their ideas. Although this can be frustrating for the person who came up with the idea, it's great for the rest of us as we benefit from the improvements made with the existing idea. Here are a few examples:

- **New business processes.** Some of the most powerful ideas involve rearranging how a company runs itself. In 1776, in the first chapter of *The Wealth of Nations*, Adam Smith marveled how an English factory divides pin making into 18 different tasks. Smith calculated that one worker, who could by himself make one pin a day, could now make 4,000. "The division of labor occasions, in every art, a proportionable increase in the productive powers of labor," he wrote. Two centuries later Walmart revolutionized retailing by using big box stores, bar codes, wireless scanning guns, and exchanging electronic information with its suppliers to track and move goods more efficiently while scheduling cashiers better to reduce slack time. As competitors like Target and Sears copied Walmart, customers of all three benefited from lower prices and more selection, a McKinsey study found.

- **New products.** Netscape's Navigator was the first commercially successful browser but was soon supplanted by Microsoft's Internet Explorer, which is now under siege by Mozilla Firefox, Apple Safari, and Google Chrome. Browsers keep getting better but consumers still pay the same price, zero. Drugs provide another example. Eli Lilly's introduction of the antidepressant Prozac in 1986 inspired competitors to develop similar drugs like Zoloft and Celexa, providing alternatives for patients who didn't respond well to Prozac.*

Ideas can be patented, or copyrighted. But overly restrictive patents and copyrights discourage the spread of ideas and leave society worse off. A lot fewer books would have been written if the estate of Johannes Gutenberg collected a fee on every one.

It's not just companies that thrive by imitating their competitors. Entire countries can turbocharge their development by strategically copying the ideas and technologies that other countries already use. Eckhard Höffner, an economic historian, attributes Germany's rapid industrial development in the nineteenth century

*According to Robin Arnold of IMS Health.

to weak copyright laws, which encouraged publishers to flood the country with cheap (and often plagiarized) copies of essential technical manuals. Japanese steelmakers didn't invent the basic oxygen furnace; they adapted it from a Swiss professor who had devised it in the 1940s. They thus leapfrogged U.S. steelmakers who were using less efficient open-hearth furnaces. Japan's mainframe computer makers benefited from a government edict that IBM make its patents available as a condition of doing business there.

More recently, China's adaptation of existing ideas from other countries has resulted in significant economic growth. Since 1978, it has moved workers from unproductive farms and state-owned companies to more productive privately owned factories that used machinery and technology bought, borrowed, and sometimes stolen from foreigners. Foreign companies are routinely required to share their expertise with local partners as a condition of doing business in China.

Still, once a country has copied all the ideas it can, future growth depends on waiting for new ideas or developing its own. Inevitably, a country at the technological frontier grows more slowly than one catching up to the frontier. As we learned earlier in this chapter, that's just what happened to Japan. It could also happen to China.

Nurturing Growth

Getting the ingredients right is essential to economic growth, but so is the environment that the government creates to foster its development. Like the temperature on the oven, the wrong setting can ruin the recipe. So, what do governments do that matters most?

- **Human capital**. It's no use equipping workers with the most advanced equipment in the world if they can't read the instructions. Education and training, both forms of human capital, are essential to productivity. Korea went from third-world status to the ranks of the industrialized nations in a generation in part by rigorously educating all its children. Its high school graduation rates now exceed those of the United States.

- **Rule of law**. Investors will invest today only if they know they get to keep the rewards years later. That requires transparent laws, impartial courts, and the right to property. The United States' army of lawyers sues at the drop of a hat and wrap every transaction in legalese, but in a maddening way that signifies its respect for laws.

 Small government is better than big government, but size is less important than quality. For

example, Sweden's government spends more than half of gross domestic product (GDP) while Mexico's spends only a quarter of its GDP. But Swedish government is efficient and honest while Mexico's is inefficient and rife with corruption. That's one reason Sweden is rich and Mexico is poor.

Is democracy necessary for growth? It helps: Governments that make people poor usually lose elections. But there's no firm rule. The authoritarian governments of China, Korea, and Chile ran smart policies that produced strong growth early in their development. Conversely, sometimes democratic governments are pressured by voters to expropriate private property, run up unsupportable debts, or shelter politically favored groups at everyone else's expense. But dictators have done all those things and worse, bringing on social unrest that ruins the investment climate. Democracy provides essential feedback to government just as free markets do to companies, and elections are generally less disruptive than civil wars.

- **Letting markets work**. Entrepreneurs and workers get rich coming up with new, cheaper ways to make things. In the process, they drive someone else out of business. Joseph Schumpeter, the

Austrian-born Harvard economist, called this "creative destruction." Governments squelch creative destruction by propping up shrinking industries, or barring the entry of new competitors. Policies that direct capital to favored sectors, such as housing in the United States, result in too much investment in unproductive activities and too little in promising, innovative enterprises. China's banks lend too much to state-owned enterprises (SOEs) and too little to private companies.

Into the Weeds

Now that we've established what a country needs to grow, how do we measure that growth? The global gold standard is gross domestic product, or GDP, the value of all the products and services a country produces in a year. GDP can be measured in two ways:

1. **Expenditure-based GDP.** Total of all the money spent on stuff.
2. **Income-based GDP.** Total of all the money earned producing stuff.

Expenditure-based GDP includes spending by consumers—on such items as houses, bread, and visits

to the doctor—and by government—on such items as schools and soldiers. It also includes spending by businesses, but only on investment-related expenses—such as a bakery's new oven or building. GDP excludes what business spends on inputs (e.g., ingredients, fuel, and parts) that go into what its customers buy. For example, when a consumer buys a cake, she is also buying the eggs and flour that the baker bought to make the cake. We include the consumer's purchase of cake in GDP but not the baker's purchase of eggs and flour as that would be counting it twice. Exports are also included in *expenditure-based GDP* because this represents what foreigners spend on things made in the United States. Imports are subtracted from GDP to exclude what Americans spend on things made in other countries.

Expenditure-based GDP is measured in nominal and real dollars. *Nominal dollars* represent the actual value of activity. *Real dollars* remove the effects of inflation. Suppose sales of bread rise 5 percent. If the price per loaf rose 2 percent, then real spending on bread (i.e., the number of loaves sold) rose 3 percent. That's real GDP and it's the usual way of measuring economic growth. However, you can't spend real GDP—wages and profits are earned in nominal dollars so nominal GDP is a better way to measure the size of the economy.

The second method, *income-based GDP*, includes the wages, benefits, and bonuses earned by workers and managers; the profits earned by companies and their shareholders; the interest earned by lenders; and the rent earned by landlords.

In theory, the expenditure-based GDP and income-based GDP should be equal, because one person's spending is another person's income. In practice, however, GDP is so large and complex that it would be a miracle if calculating it two ways produced the same number.

When the U.S. Commerce Department's Bureau of Economic Analysis calculates GDP, 75 percent of its initial estimate is based on surveys of actual activity like retail sales and construction. For the rest it gets creative. For example, it checks out the weather to estimate utility output or dog registrations to estimate spending at veterinarians' offices. It sounds goofy, but it lines up pretty well with the hard data that eventually replaces it.

GDP is not the same as well-being. As Robert Kennedy* noted in 1968, it includes "special locks for our doors and the jails for the people who break them" but not "the health of our children, the quality of their

*Kennedy at the time was talking about gross national product, which is similar to GDP.

education, or the joy of their play." In 2008 the French government asked prominent economists to come up with a better way to measure happiness and social progress. Still, as long as people and governments measure economic success in material terms, GDP will be their favorite yardstick.

Will the United States Become the Next Japan?

In 2007 the United States sank into its eleventh, and worst, recession since World War II. It emerged in 2009 but the ensuing expansion has been slow and halting. Unemployment declined much more slowly than after the previous worst recessions, those of 1973 to 1975 and 1981 to 1982. After inflation, household incomes were lower in 2011 than a decade earlier. Pessimism about America's prospects is pervasive: In one poll more Americans thought the twenty-first century would be a Chinese century rather than an American century.

Is the pessimism warranted? China's per-person income is only a tenth of America's but because it has more than four times as many people, its economy is almost half as large. When China's per-person income passes a quarter of America's, its economy will be larger. Because productivity in China is rising so quickly and the value of its currency is rising against the dollar that point will probably be reached by the end of this decade.

That is not a sign of American decline but of China exploiting the time-tested recipe of education, urbanization, and industrialization to graduate from poor- to middle-income status. Many countries like Mexico have done the same, only to stumble before becoming rich. To avoid the same trap, China has a delicate transition: Having grown through exports, investment, and manufacturing it must now rely more on services and consumers, which are less easily steered by government overseers.

What about America? As female baby boomers put their child-bearing years behind them and older boomers retire, its population and labor force will grow more slowly. Nonetheless, America's relatively high fertility rate and immigration means its population will grow more quickly than that of almost any developed country for some years to come.

The real question mark is whether Americans will keep generating new ideas and investing in them so that productivity can keep rising. Some signposts are troubling; the technology bubble of the 1990s left the United States with broadband Internet and business-to-business websites. By contrast, the real estate bubble of the late-2000s left behind vacant houses and bad property loans that made it harder for the businesses of tomorrow to get money.

In 2012, Americans expressed less faith in free markets than did Brazilians and Chinese. Government has grown: There are more rules now governing health care, the environment, and finance. Yet America's model is not broken. The business insurgents who drive creative destruction still get a warmer welcome in America than anywhere else; from Amazon.com to Google to Facebook, the companies most likely to topple the established economic order were born in the United States. Americans are jaded about finance but still like free enterprise. In April 2009, at the depths of the worst recession and bear market in memory, the Pew Research Center found that 90 percent of Americans said they admired people who get rich by working hard. Optimists would also point out that American legal and democratic traditions have survived intact. Populist anger at bankers helped produce both the Tea Party and Occupy Wall Street movements. Yet in the first major criminal trial stemming from the mortgage meltdown, jurors acquitted two traders for Bear Stearns, because, one said, "We just didn't have enough to convict them."

The optimist would go on to note that for all the rhetoric to the contrary, U.S. leaders still believe in free enterprise, as well. Within three years of taking stakes in nine major banks, the Treasury had sold all of them.

True, the federal government propped up General Motors; but to get the money GM had to go through bankruptcy and shear off 30 percent of its U.S. workforce. By contrast, France gave money to Peugeot and Renault only after they promised to preserve French jobs. In 2011, GM recorded record profits.

If the financial system can flush the bad debt left from the property bubble, then investment should resume and with it, productivity growth of perhaps 1.5 percent to 2 percent per year. Add that to labor force growth of 0.75 percent and you get long-term growth of 2.25 percent to 2.75 percent per year. The United States may no longer be a glamorous growth stock, but it's still a blue chip.

The Bottom Line

- Long-term economic growth depends on population and productivity. A growing population is the source of future workers, and the more productive those workers are, the richer they become. It takes investment in both capital and ideas to raise productivity.

- Ideas enable us to recombine the workers and the capital we already have in new ways to produce brand-new products, or old products at a lower price. Competition forces countries and companies to copy each other's ideas and constantly come up with new ones.

- Both investment and ideas must be nurtured. Honest government and trustworthy laws encourage investors and innovators to take risks in hopes of reaping the rewards. Investment in education enables workers to take advantage of the latest ideas. And free markets ensure that dying, unproductive industries are culled so that growing industries can attract capital and workers.

Chapter Two

Economic
Bungee Jumping

~

*Business Cycles, Recessions, and
Depressions . . . Oh My!*

IN EARLY 1973 THE *New York Times* asked four economists for their forecasts. Alan Greenspan predicted that the economy would grow 6 percent and declared, "It's very rare that you can be as unqualifiedly bullish as you can now." He was half right; the economy did grow 6 percent that year, but it was a lousy time to be bullish.

A few days after the *Times* article appeared, stocks entered a deep, multiyear bear market and by the end of the year the economy had fallen into its worst recession in decades.

What happened? Economic growth and falling unemployment began to strain the economy's productive capacity. Inflation was rising and soon, so were interest rates. That October came the *coup de grâce*: The Arab embargo sent oil prices skyrocketing. High interest rates and recession are a nasty combination for stocks and employment.

Over long stretches, the economy grows thanks to rising population and productivity. But in the short run, it goes through cycles of expansion and recession. Catching the bottom of the cycle can turbocharge your portfolio or business plan, while missing the peak can lay waste to both.

Medicine has made countless breakthroughs that enable us to live longer, healthier lives, but it hasn't yet eradicated epidemics. For the same reason, both our wealth and our understanding of the economy have advanced tremendously but we haven't yet abolished the business cycle. Business cycles are an unavoidable and largely unpredictable feature of market economies.

Business cycles and market cycles have a lot in common. Both are driven in great part by a tug-of-war

between expectations and reality. Just as stock prices are a bet on the future of companies that may prove wrong, businesses and households are constantly making plans based on how much they expect their sales or wages to grow. The future is inherently uncertain, so these decisions often depend as much on gut feelings as cold calculation. Expectations are heavily shaped by the recent past. If video games sold well last month, a store will order more this month. If home prices rose sharply last year, builders will build more homes this year.

Business cycles and market cycles reinforce each other. As General Electric or eBay report rising profits, investors bid their stocks to nosebleed levels. When cash flow and asset prices rise, fewer borrowers default so investors buy more corporate bonds and subprime mortgages. Higher stock prices make CEOs think they are geniuses, so they expand their businesses further. Easy credit tempts both businesses and consumers to borrow more than they can safely handle.

∼

**Every business expansion eventually dies.
Only the cause of death changes.**

These imbalances inevitably unwind. Just as people often get sick faster than they get better, bear markets

are more violent than bull markets and unemployment rises more quickly than it falls. The event that ends these imbalances and thus the business cycle is seldom the same. In nineteenth-century America, it was often a natural disaster, a crop failure, or a bank panic. In 1973 and 1990, it was a spike in oil prices. In 2001, technology investments crashed. In 2007, house values plummeted. We sometimes think we'll eliminate recessions if we could just inoculate ourselves against past imbalances. After all, we can develop immunity to the last virus we contracted. The problem is that it mutates and we're susceptible all over again. The same holds true for the business cycle. Every business expansion eventually dies. Only the cause of death changes.

Not Your Father's Business Cycle

There is one common element to almost all modern business cycles. As the economist Rudi Dornbusch wrote in 1998, "None of the post-war expansions died of natural causes, they were all murdered by the Fed."

The Federal Reserve raises interest rates if it thinks the economy is growing so fast that inflation will rise. Costlier credit eventually forces businesses and consumers to curb their spending—sometimes abruptly. Long ago, the effect was brutally direct. Regulation Q, a rule passed during the Depression, limited how much

interest banks could pay on deposits. When the Fed tightened monetary policy, interest rates in the financial markets rose more than on bank deposits. As a result, people shifted money out of their saving accounts and into higher-yielding money market funds. As deposits shrank, banks had to curtail lending. Sales of homes and cars, which are often bought on credit, shriveled. Companies suddenly found inventories piling up and had to shut down production and lay off workers. Laid-off workers slashed their own spending, multiplying the initial impact. Recession ensued.

Happily, the Fed could also end recessions by cutting interest rates. And, like a bungee jump, the deeper the dive, the sharper the upswing. People who had put off buying houses, cars, and other large-ticket items troop back to the stores. Companies with too little inventory on hand restart production and hire back workers. Those workers spend anew, which leads to more hiring and the expansion becomes self-supporting.

Business cycles changed after 1982. Inflation became better behaved, so the Fed did not raise interest rates as much or as often. Innovation and deregulation weakened Regulation Q so when interest rates rose, banks could still make loans. *Just-in-time* management ensured inventories didn't get far out of line with sales, while a growing chunk of gross domestic product (GDP) went toward

services like knee surgery and yoga lessons that don't require inventories. The Fed seemed omnipotent: It nimbly raised interest rates before inflation broke out, and cut them before growth crumbled. The two recessions that did occur, 1990 to 1991 and 2001, were uncommonly mild. Economists dubbed this era the *Great Moderation*.

Alas, neither business cycles nor imbalances had been tamed; they simply changed shape. Hyman Minsky, an unorthodox, wild-haired economist largely ignored by his colleagues before his death in 1996, had argued that capitalism was inherently unstable and periods of stability would simply result in even bigger imbalances that ultimately come undone in a turbulent crisis or recession—something his followers dubbed a *Minsky Moment*. The 25-year Great Moderation encouraged everyone to take on more debt, hold less cash, and pay more for homes and other assets on the belief the business cycle had been tamed. The financial crisis of 2007 to 2009 was a classic Minsky Moment, when expectations were brutally brought back to earth.

Predicting recessions is all about spotting imbalances, such as a rising ratio of inventories to sales of big-ticket goods or a growing backlog of unbuilt office towers as vacancy rates rise. Yet an imbalance can last a long time, or may be corrected without bringing the entire economy down. Economists and policy makers

often miss fatal imbalances because they're looking in the wrong place. Having vaccinated everyone against whatever killed the last business cycle, they fail to spot the virus that infects the current one.

Ringing the Gong

How do you know a recession has occurred? Easy: a press release goes out. In 1920, a group of academics formed the National Bureau of Economic Research (NBER) to promote better economic analysis.

Since 1978, the NBER has entrusted business cycle dating to a committee of six to eight of its scholars. They periodically examine a bunch of indicators— manufacturing shipments, wholesale trade, income, industrial production, employment. They declare a recession when they conclude there has been "a significant decline in economic activity spread across the economy, lasting more than a few months."

Because the declaration of the start and end of a recession comes many months after the fact, it's about as useful to investors as an autopsy is to an emergency room physician. The NBER would rather be right than early. Theirs is not the only definition of recession out there; it's simply the most popular. Sometimes recession is defined as two or more consecutive quarters of declining GDP. This is not very practical, though, because

GDP is often revised. Therefore, under this definition, a recession, like a Cheshire cat, might disappear, reappear, and change shape.

When the Bungee Cord Breaks

In June 1930, some bankers and religious leaders visited Herbert Hoover to air their concerns about the economy. "Gentlemen, you have come 60 days too late," he told them. "The depression is over." Actually, it would run for almost three more years.

At the time, *depression* was the term used for what we now call a *recession*. Since then, the word is reserved for a slump of calamitous proportions.

Depressions occur when the economy's normal recuperative mechanism fails to engage.

Depressions are like plagues: devastating, rare, and only dimly understood until after the fact. They occur when the economy's normal recuperative mechanism fails to engage; the bungee cord breaks. The usual

culprit is a broken financial system. Often, an investment boom turns to bust, leaving businesses and consumers with a glut of unneeded buildings and equipment that depresses future spending. The loans they took out to finance their investment go bad, crippling banks and leaving borrowers unable to get money even at rock-bottom interest rates. If lower interest rates can't stimulate demand, the virtuous circle of spending, job creation, and rising incomes can't begin.

Like recessions, depressions have no official definition. Harry Truman said "a recession [is] when your neighbor loses his job; it's a depression when you lose yours." One rule of thumb, according to the *Economist*, is that a depression is a contraction in economic activity of at least 10 percent or lasting at least three years. By that standard, the last one in the United States was from 1929 to 1933. Perhaps that lulled Americans into thinking we'd eradicated depressions, but a look to other countries would have proved otherwise. Finland's GDP shrank 10 percent between 1989 and 1993 thanks to the collapse of the Soviet Union, a major trading partner, and its banks. Indonesia's GDP shrank 13 percent in 1998 after its economy and financial system collapsed. Between 2008 and 2011, Greece's GDP shriveled by 13 percent as it bore the brunt of the euro crisis.

Financial crises don't always produce depressions, but they often lead to severe recessions with unusually weak recoveries. That's because the assets acquired during the boom collapse in value, but the debt doesn't: it must still be repaid. The stagnation that followed the collapse of Japanese stock and land prices in the early 1990s is an example. Many Japanese companies were left insolvent, meaning their debts far exceeded their assets, and were determined to pay down debt, a process called *deleveraging*. If people or companies can't or won't borrow, then even rock-bottom interest rates won't spur the usual burst of spending.

The same problem afflicted the United States after home prices plunged 32 percent between the end of 2006 and 2011. Three years after the recession ended in 2009, almost a quarter of homeowners with mortgages still owed more than their houses were worth. Such people usually can't get a new loan, and many don't want to borrow anyway. A country convalescing from a crisis often falls back into recession. Just as a plane flying close to the ground is more likely to crash, a slow-growing economy succumbs more easily to a shock: a spike in oil prices, or a major trading partner's recession. Governments often run up big debts dealing with crises and when they try to whittle them back by cutting spending or raising taxes, they may inadvertently

cause a recession. Britain, like the United States, suffered a severe crisis and recession in 2008, and its recovery was tepid. In late 2011, it fell back into recession, a victim of turmoil in Europe, which is a major customer, deleveraging business and government deficit cuts.

The good news is that the scars of even the most devastating recessions eventually fade. America had depressions in the 1870s and 1930s but both eventually gave way to new booms. Japan has not yet put its debts behind it; nonetheless, by 2006 it was growing respectably, though the global financial crisis and a 2011 earthquake then set it back. Millions of Americans defaulted and lost their homes during and after the Great Recession, but that speeds up deleveraging. Eventually, America will again grow normally, until some new, unseen misfortune knocks it down again.

The Bottom Line

- Ultimately, long-run growth drives our standard of living. In the short run, the economy goes through regular cycles of expansion and recession. These cycles are driven by how much consumers and businesses spend, which in turn depends a lot on their view of the future.

- Bullish expectations boost investment, stock prices, and lending, all of which feed back to the economy.

Eventually, though, expectations get ahead of fundamentals, creating imbalances. These imbalances come undone, usually with a nudge from the Federal Reserve, producing recessions.

- Recessions create pent-up demand. Lower interest rates eventually release that demand, bringing the recession to a close. Sometimes, though, this natural recuperative process fails, because a broken financial system dams the flow of credit. Then, a recession may become a depression.

Chapter Three

In-Flight Monitor

—— ∼ ——

*Tracking and Forecasting
the Business Cycle from Takeoff
to Landing*

ON A COAST-TO-COAST flight you can relax with a drink and watch your progress on the video monitor in front of you, up to the minute you descend into your destination city. Wouldn't it be nice if we could do the same with the economy: Flip on a screen and know instantly where the economy is, how fast it's growing, and whether a recession lies ahead.

Unfortunately, when you clamber into the economy's cockpit you discover erratic and imprecise instruments, a filthy windshield, and outdated, faded maps. Still, imperfect though they are, we have a wealth of data and tools with which to track the economy's journey.

The Four Engines of the Economy

The most popular way of tracking the economy is by looking at its four principal categories of spending. If the economy is an airplane, then its four engines are consumers, businesses, government, and exports. Its speed depends on the power of all of these engines. However, these engines aren't all the same size and they operate at different speeds. Below are their average shares of total GDP from 2007 through 2011. They total more than 100 percent of the gross domestic product (GDP), because imports are subtracted from GDP.

- Consumer spending on goods and services: 70 percent.
- On housing, apartments and renovations 3 percent.
- Business investment in buildings: 3 percent.
- In equipment: 8 percent.
- Investment in inventories: zero.
- Government spending: 19 percent.

- Exports: 12 percent.
- Imports: minus 16 percent.

Consumer spending represents the largest engine on the airplane, accounting for about two-thirds of GDP. It is primarily driven by household income; when wages and jobs go up, spending usually follows. It is also driven by wealth. When home prices or stocks go up a lot, consumers feel wealthier and spend more: Typically, a dollar more of wealth boosts spending by four cents that year. Conversely, when home prices and stocks drop, consumers spend less and the economy weakens.

Consumer spending is also driven by the ephemeral role of confidence. The more fearful consumers are for the future, the less they spend. Sounds obvious, right? But, sometimes the obvious is wrong. The Conference Board and the University of Michigan conduct confidence surveys but they aren't great predictors of what consumers actually do. Consumers were traumatized by the terrorist attacks of September 11, 2001, but when car companies rolled out mouthwatering zero percent financing shortly thereafter, they jumped.

Consumer spending is the economy's ballast: Though large, it doesn't fluctuate much from quarter to quarter, except for big-ticket purchases like houses and

cars. Paychecks and Social Security checks are fairly steady and consumers try to spend the same each month on groceries, tuition, and medical premiums.

Although housing is a type of consumer spending, it behaves differently from the rest. Though one of the smallest contributors to GDP it's historically been one of the most volatile. Over time, it follows demographic forces like population, family size, immigration, and the demand for vacation homes. But because a house is such a big commitment and so sensitive to interest rates, it's the first thing consumers postpone when interest rates rise or they lose their jobs.

From the late 1990s until 2006, demand for homes outstripped demographic forces thanks to low mortgage rates, reduced down payment requirements, and the spread of "subprime" mortgages, which borrowers with less than stellar credit could obtain. Young families bought homes earlier than their parents did while speculators bought homes they never planned to live in. Since houses are the collateral for mortgages, their rising prices made mortgages seem safer and thus lenders were more eager to offer them. Rising prices naturally encouraged more supply. New suburbs sprang up outside most major cities such as Maricopa, southwest of Phoenix, which grew from 329 houses in 2000 to 15,000 later that decade. In 1995, 64 percent of

American households owned their own home; by 2006, 69 percent did.

When home prices began to fall, those forces switched into reverse. Lenders once issued mortgages to people who could fog a mirror; after 2007, they required mountains of documentation and tough new standards of income and credit. Housing's share of the economy shrank.

After consumers, business investment is the next most important component of GDP. It comes in three types: inventories, buildings, or equipment. Businesses accumulate inventories either on purpose to meet future sales, or by accident because sales drop off unexpectedly. Investment in inventories can actually be negative. Suppose a business starts the quarter with 10 widgets and ends with 6: Spending on widgets must have exceeded production by 4. Recording that drop in inventories as negative investment ensures that total spending equals total production. When firms can't match production to sudden shifts in demand, they let inventories pile up (a positive contribution to GDP), or run down (a negative contribution). Switching from positive in one quarter to less positive in the next, or even negative, can have a big impact on the change in GDP. But over time, as businesses restore inventories to comfortable levels, the positives and negatives cancel out.

Numerous factors influence how businesses invest in buildings and equipment: stronger profits, higher stock prices, lower interest rates, and the potential profitability of the investment. In the early 2000s, many airlines were bankrupt yet went ahead and installed thousands of high-tech self-serve ticketing kiosks in airports around the world, because they issued tickets at 5 percent of the cost of using an agent.

Regulations affect investment by altering its potential profitability. Federal restrictions on emissions of nitrogen oxide, sulphur dioxide and carbon dioxide have made coal-burning power plants more expensive to operate and thus fewer are being built. Uncertainty also affects investment. In the years it takes an investment to pay off, a lot of things can go wrong: A new competitor could enter the market, customers could change their tastes, a natural disaster or terrorist attack could disrupt production, the government could impose new rules, or relax existing ones. The more uncertain a business is of these things, the higher a return it will need to justify an investment.

By far the most important driver of business investment, and the biggest source of uncertainty, is the sales outlook. If consumer demand is growing briskly, businesses will expand to meet that demand. And when consumers pull back, so, eventually, will businesses. In fact, because months or even years may elapse between the

decision to add a factory, store, or product line and the completion of the project, investment is kind of an accelerator, pushing the economy farther both on the way up and on the way down. In 2004, amidst an oil-fueled boom, bullish developers in the Persian Gulf emirate of Dubai broke ground on the world's tallest skyscraper. By the time the rocket-shape half-mile tall edifice was completed in early 2010, Dubai was deeply mired in recession and on the verge of default.

What government spends on actual services and supplies, such as tanks, teachers, and park rangers, shows up in GDP, but not when it simply transfers money to people—such as Social Security benefits and bond interest. That money only affects GDP when the recipient spends it.

Exports represent what foreigners spend on stuff produced domestically, so they are added to GDP. Imports, however, are domestic spending on things produced by foreigners. Suppose consumers spend $100 more on imported food. GDP will show both consumer spending and imports going up by $100. Treating imports as a negative ensures the net impact on GDP is zero.

These main economic engines can all be monitored in the quarterly GDP figures. There are also numerous other economic indicators that offer more detailed views of the economy. The following are some of the most

important. (I discuss employment, inflation, and trade in later chapters.)

- **Manufacturing**. A legacy of the United States' industrialized past is that we have a lot of manufacturing data. Each month the Census Bureau reports shipments, orders, and inventories of durable goods (goods designed to last at least three years). An important subsector of durable goods is capital goods, such as machine tools and computers. Capital goods orders are a good guide to business investment, although before you draw any conclusions you should exclude aircraft and defense orders: They're so volatile they muddy the underlying trend. The Census Bureau separately reports total factory orders, which (besides durable goods) covers nondurables, such as packaged food and gasoline. Each month the Federal Reserve reports industrial production, and the private Institute for Supply Management (ISM) releases an index of manufacturing activity based on a survey of purchasing managers.
- **Real estate**. The Census Bureau issues three key monthly real estate reports. The first covers housing starts—the number of new homes on which construction begins—and building permits,

which, like starts, track construction but are less affected by weather. A second report covers sales and prices of newly built homes. A third report covers construction spending, from hospitals and highways to apartment buildings and stores. The National Association of Realtors reports the number of existing homes sold and the median price every month. The Federal Housing Finance Agency and S&P/Case-Shiller issue separate monthly reports on home prices.

- **Consumer spending**. The Census Bureau reports retail sales each month. Sales of automobiles are volatile and gasoline's price seesaws, so if you want the underlying trend you should exclude these categories. Retail sales cover only 40 percent of consumer spending because services and housing are excluded. Once a month, the Bureau of Economic Analysis reports total consumer spending and its major components, which include services and durable goods. It also records personal income and saving.

The Mapmakers

When you set out on a journey you are at the mercy of the people who draw your maps. When you track the

economy, you have to trust the people who gather the statistics. Collecting these numbers is a core duty of government, although it hasn't always been. In 1884 the *New York Times* greeted the creation of what is now the Bureau of Labor Statistics as "a fine bit of Congressional witlessness."

Three federal agencies produce the lion's share of our economic data: the Bureau of Economic Analysis (BEA) and the Census Bureau, both part of the Commerce Department, and the Bureau of Labor Statistics (BLS) in the Labor Department. The Federal Reserve also produces some data, such as industrial production and consumer credit. Last, private organizations like the National Association of Realtors and the Conference Board produce some key data.

~

U.S. politicians certainly abuse statistics but virtually never interfere with them.

In some countries, governments regularly interfere with economic statistics. For instance, since 2007, Argentina has regularly tampered with how it measures consumer prices. It claimed inflation in early 2012 was 10 percent when a private firm estimated it was 24

percent. The Chinese government frequently reports suspect data—growth reported by the provinces often differs from what the central government reports for the whole country. (In recent years, because of outside scrutiny, Chinese statistics have gotten better.) Garbage in, garbage out: Bad data leads investors and businesses to make bad decisions. At the extreme, it undermines trust in government.

U.S. politicians certainly abuse statistics but virtually never interfere with them. The statistical agencies, though run by political appointees, are independent and apolitical. Even so, the data isn't perfect. The agencies track the economy by sampling people and businesses; then they extrapolate the data and apply it to the whole economy. That's an imprecise science given how big, varied, and ever-changing the economy is. As with opinion polls, data surveys have their margins of error, and some are quite large, leading to large revisions later on when more data is available. For instance, the Census Bureau estimates new home sales from a small sample of local permit offices based on building patterns that may be decades old. The margin of error in these surveys is usually around 20 percent, and numbers are routinely revised up or down by 5 percent. Revisions can cast economic history in a different light. The Bureau of Economic Analysis announced in 2011 that the

economy had shrunk far more in 2008 and 2009 than it had first said. Had policy makers known that, at the time, they may have enacted stronger stimulus.

Data is often seasonally adjusted to help see through patterns that recur each year. It is pretty useless to learn that retail sales rose from November to December: They always do, typically by about 17 percent. They then fall back in January. What we want to know is: Did they rise by more than usual? That's what seasonal adjustment does: It removes predictable calendar effects. If retail sales only rose 15 percent in December, that would be a disappointing drop of 2 percent, seasonally adjusted.

All these procedures mean our data is never perfect; but nor is it dishonest or biased. You can generally assume that, if there are errors, they cancel each other out over time.

How to Make Astrologers Look Prescient

Economists pore over all this data and more and combine it into a forecast of where the economy is going. Their success rate is the stuff of comedy. John Kenneth Galbraith once remarked that "The only function of economic forecasting is to make astrology look respectable." Alan Murray of the *Wall Street Journal* once quipped, "If pilots' vision were as bad as economists',

Amtrak would be profitable." In 2006, not one of the
economists surveyed by the *Wall Street Journal* pre-
dicted a recession.

\sim

Lots of detailed economic forecasts are
available for free (though remember:
Advice is worth what you pay for it!).

 Truth be told, forecasts aren't useless: Indeed, the
average of a group of forecasts is more accurate than
simply assuming next year will be like this year. For all
the well-earned ridicule, economists are still in demand
by businesses, governments, and investors who prefer a
bad forecast to no forecast. Even a wrong forecast sheds
light on the behavior of the economy and helps us reca-
librate our decisions.

 Lots of detailed economic forecasts are available for
free (though remember: Advice is worth what you pay
for it!). The *Wall Street Journal* surveys about 50
forecasters each month and publishes their views online
at wsj.com/economist. The *Economist* surveys econo-
mists once a month and publishes either their projec-
tions or those of its sister forecasting organization, the

Economist Intelligence Unit. They appear each week for about 40 countries in its second-to-last page and at www.economist.com/markets-data. The International Monetary Fund, the Congressional Budget Office, the Organisation for Economic Co-operation and Development, and the Conference Board all publish regular, unbiased forecasts.

Of the many leading indicators you can look to, financial markets are among the best. Investors are constantly sifting millions of bits of new information—from corporate earnings to the corn harvest—and what they learn is instantly reflected in the prices of shares, commodities, and bonds. The stock market will often signal a turn in the economy 1 to 12 months ahead of time. When bond yields are equal to or below the Fed's interest rate target, producing a flat or inverted yield curve, a recession is usually one to two years away. This is obviously less useful when short-term rates are at zero. Investors are a moody bunch so stocks and interest rates often send false signals. Paul Samuelson, a Nobel Prize–winning economist, once joked that the stock market has forecast nine of the past five recessions. Remember the stock market crash of 1987? The next recession was still three years away.

The Bottom Line

- The four engines of economic growth are consumer spending, business investment, government spending, and exports. Consumers are, by far, the largest contributor to GDP.

- Movements in GDP are dominated by the most volatile categories of spending: housing, business inventories, and big-ticket consumer purchases, like cars.

- Forecasting the business cycle is risky business; you have to carefully monitor a continuous blizzard of data, which, though faithfully gathered, may be out of date and inaccurate. Stock prices, the yield curve, and commodity prices are all useful leading indicators but send a lot of error signals.

Labor Pains

~

Employment, Unemployment, and Wages

TRY TO IMAGINE A worse time to start a new career. The world is in the grip of its worst recession since the 1930s. The prime minister of Canada proclaims, "We are moving from crisis to catastrophe." The U.S. unemployment rate is at its highest since the Great Depression.

That was what the world looked like in 1982 when Howard Schultz told his mother he was quitting his job as a well-paid salesman to join a five-store chain of

coffee shops. No wonder she tried to change his mind. "You have a future," she pleaded. "Don't give it up for a small company nobody's ever heard of." Schultz ignored her, and millions of caffeine addicts are glad he did: He went on to turn Starbucks into a multinational franchise with more than 16,000 stores and well over 100,000 employees around the world while introducing a new job title into the American lexicon: *barista*.

Howard Schultz probably didn't spend a lot of time in 1982 trying to figure out how he'd keep more than 100,000 people employed in 30 years' time. That's the beauty of the job machine. In the depths of recession it is almost impossible to conceive of where the jobs will come from. Yet the new jobs always come.

Say It Ain't So

When people wonder "Where will the jobs come from?" they reflect a popular anxiety.

Two centuries ago, Jean-Baptiste Say, a French economist, elegantly argued that there can never be too little work to go around. If a waiter earns $25 by working two hours longer, he'll spend the $25 on something, or put it in the bank, which then lends it to someone to spend. That $25 in extra demand is exactly enough to pay for what he supplied with his extra labor. Say's law dictates that "Supply creates its own demand."

Some economists go so far as to argue that anyone who is unemployed must therefore not really want to work, at least for the wages available. Common sense tells us this isn't true. In a recession, an unemployed worker who offered to work for half the going wage would get few offers. When a recession cuts sales, firms stop hiring, cut hours, or lay off workers . They do not fire their existing workers and hire new ones at half the wage.

But over time a healthy economy should always create enough jobs to employ the people available to work. Since 1982, the number of working-age Americans who want to work has grown 39 percent, or about 43 million. Back in 1982, who could imagine what all those people would do? Yet they found jobs, injecting enough money back into the economy to maintain the demand for their labor. In the same period, the number of jobs has grown an almost identical 42 million, or 46 percent.

Diving into the Employment Petri Dish

Assessing the health of the labor market starts with figuring out just how big it is. Some of the working-age population, those aged 16 to 65, are in school, at home raising children, in prison, in the military, or have retired. The share of the working-age population either working

or looking for work is called the labor force participation rate.

But participation fluctuates a lot from month to month, often depending on business conditions. In recessions, some of the unemployed may decide not to look for work. These jobless workers are not counted as unemployed. Participation also changes with society. When *Leave It to Beaver* was on the air in the 1950s, less than 40 percent of working-age women were in the labor force. By the time *Murphy Brown* went off the airwaves in 1998, 60 percent were. It's no coincidence that the participation rate that year hit an all-time high of 67 percent.

The participation rate has since declined, falling quite sharply after 2007, to 64 percent in 2011. With fewer people looking for jobs, the unemployment rate fell more quickly. Had participation not fallen, then unemployment would have been 12 percent in 2011 instead of 9 percent.

What's behind this exodus of workers? Many aging baby boomers have retired early. More young people are going to college. And some of the unemployed have given up looking for work altogether, choosing instead to retire, collect disability, or stay home with their children.

—————— ∿ ——————

**The job market is a wonderfully chaotic
Petri dish, in which new jobs are constantly
being created or destroyed.**

The monthly change in jobs garners huge headlines but it is just the tip of the iceberg. The job market is a wonderfully chaotic Petri dish, in which new jobs are constantly being created or destroyed as new firms grow and old firms die. In 2007, when the economy was humming, about 2 million people were fired or laid off each month and almost 3 million more quit their jobs. This loss of jobs was just offset by almost 5 million people hired each month, and so net employment rose.

So, who does the hiring and firing? *Small* companies destroy just as many jobs as they create; they aren't disproportionate job creators. By contrast, new companies do create a surprisingly large share of new jobs. A 2009 study by Dane Stangler and Robert Litan of the Kauffman Foundation found that, if you took out firms that were five years old or younger, employment would contract most months. So job creation tends to be primarily the product of entrepreneurs who have a crazy

idea for starting a new company. But it's a mug's game trying to figure out which of the hundreds of thousands of start-ups each year will grow to be the big employer. In 1968, would you have bet on Fairchild Semiconductor, the giant, innovative Silicon Valley pioneer, or the two executives who left to start Intel?

Payday

So the number of jobs, over time, depends first and foremost on the number of people who want to work. But what determines how much they make?

Real pay, that is, after inflation, ultimately depends on productivity. The more a worker produces for his employer, the more he'll earn. Over time, as companies have equipped their workers with more and better equipment, their pay has risen. Someone with a backhoe can dig more than someone with a shovel, so he should earn more.

But this is not an iron law. When a worker becomes more productive, he may not be the one who benefits. A backhoe is a big investment and the increased revenue its productivity makes possible may go to the company to recover that investment, not the operator. If he doesn't have much bargaining power, his employer may leave his salary alone while racking up higher profits. More often, the customer benefits. Newspaper

reporters are a lot more productive now because an article they once wrote just for the newspaper now also reaches thousands of more readers on the web. The problem is that most newspapers can't persuade online readers to pay for the articles. So the benefit of the reporter's increased productivity goes principally to readers who get news for free, while the reporter may have to take a pay cut!

Wages have become a lot more unequal in recent decades. This isn't because of racial or sexual discrimination. In fact, while white men do earn more than women and minority men, the gap has been closing. The disparity these days is based on education and skills. Imagine everyone standing on a 10-rung ladder, with the lowest paid on the bottom rung and the best paid on the top. The ladder has gotten a lot taller—those one rung from the top earned 33 percent more in 2011 than they did in 1979. But the distance between the rungs has grown, with the result that the middle rung was only 8 percent higher and the bottom rung was actually 2 percent lower.

It turns out that the rung you stand on depends a lot on how much education you have received. In the 1950s, the average high school graduate could find a job in manufacturing, railroads, construction, and other industries that were highly productive, didn't face much

foreign competition, and paid well. Over the decades, though, machines and software replaced many of those jobs. As international trade grew, U.S. workers faced competition from lower-paid workers in other countries. Services grew rapidly, and many of those jobs required either almost no skills (operating a cash register in a fast-food restaurant) or a great deal of skill (performing a heart transplant or teaching autistic children). In 1979, a person with a graduate degree earned an average 71 percent more than another person with just a high school diploma, according to the Economic Policy Institute. By 2011, that premium had leaped to 129 percent.

Education, though, can't fully explain why those at the very top have gotten so fabulously rich. Even among college graduates, inequality has grown with those at the top pulling away from the middle. According to Emmanuel Saez, an economist at the University of California, Berkeley, the 1 percent richest households

Technology and globalization have enabled celebrity athletes, singers, and corporate executives to multiply their earning power astronomically.

reaped 24 percent of all income in 2007, the highest share since 1928. In 2010, that had dropped to 20 percent. Technology and globalization have enabled celebrity athletes, singers, and corporate executives to multiply their earning power astronomically. Susan Boyle got her start singing in church and at karaoke pubs. When she sang the same songs on *Britain's Got Talent* and on bestselling CDs, her income skyrocketed.

Unemployment, Naturally

No single number better captures the health of the economy than the unemployment rate. It represents the share of the labor force that is looking for work but cannot find it. To keep the unemployment rate from rising, employment must do more than just stay the same; it has to grow as fast as the labor force. For the unemployment rate to drop, employment must grow faster than the labor force.

According to the Congressional Budget Office (CBO), the labor force grew 1 percent per year in the United States during the 2000s. Because people are always joining and quitting the labor force, some months it would grow by half a million and other months it would fall by as much. But, on average, the labor force grew by 120,000 people per month. That meant employment had to grow by more than that for

unemployment to fall. If, instead, it grew just 80,000, then the additional 40,000 would show up as unemployed and the unemployment rate would rise.

In the coming decade, the labor force will grow more slowly because, as we have seen, the population is aging and women's participation in the labor force has stopped rising. The number of new jobs we need each month to keep unemployment from rising is now around 80,000, instead of 120,000.

Yet, even in a healthy economy, it is normal for there to be some unemployment. Someone who has been fired, laid off, or has just told her boss to take this job and shove it doesn't usually take the first thing that comes along. Instead, she spends time trying to find the dream job.

Some people also struggle to find work even in a healthy economy because of a disability, poor English, or too little education. Many people are simply victims of creative destruction. A mainframe computer programmer laid off after 20 years first looks for another job programming mainframes. If the entire world has moved to personal computers, he may be out of work a long time unless he retrains or changes careers.

For all these reasons, even in an economy running at full-tilt unemployment won't drop below a minimum natural rate.

It seems cruel to label something like unemployment as *natural*, so economists also call this the *nonaccelerating inflation rate of unemployment*, or NAIRU, because below this level, firms have to jack up pay to attract qualified workers. Those higher wages eventually lead to higher prices and inflation.

The natural rate of unemployment is to economics what black holes are to physics: We know it's there but we can't really see it. It's hard to know if someone is unemployed because no one is hiring or because he simply doesn't have the necessary skills. The natural rate also moves around as the economy changes. In the early 1970s, lots of young baby boomers entered the labor force. They had less skill and experience than their parents, so they took longer to find work, which raised the natural unemployment rate.

Government policies can also affect the natural unemployment rate. Generous welfare or unemployment insurance enable workers to take longer looking for jobs while minimum wages make some unskilled workers too expensive to hire.

Many European countries make it expensive to fire workers, which makes companies think twice about hiring them in the first place. In Spain, wages are set through national or regional agreements, making it difficult to adjust pay to local conditions. A permanent

worker who is sacked can appeal, earn salary during the appeal, and 45 days' wages if the dismissal is ruled unjustified, as it usually is. The result: A quarter of Spanish workers are on temporary contracts, get little training, and are the first fired in a downturn. These rigidities amplified the effect of Spain's recessions in 2009 and 2012, pushing its unemployment rate to one of the world's highest and leaving half its youth out of work.

Into the Weeds

On the first Friday of every month, investors and politicians hold their breath, waiting for the federal Bureau of Labor Statistics (BLS) to report how the job market performed the previous month. The numbers can send stocks and bonds soaring or plunging, and unleash a torrent of press releases in Washington as the president grabs credit if it's good news and his opponents heap blame on him if it's bad.

The employment report is actually two reports.

1. In the payroll survey, the BLS surveys private and government employers in order to estimate the total number of workers on nonfarm payrolls, their hourly wages, and hours they worked. Its initial sample covers 30 percent of all U.S. workers; it estimates the rest. The BLS revises those

estimates over the following months as it gets data from more of its sample. Those revisions can be big. A new restaurant may open, then close six months later without the BLS knowing it existed. The BLS tries to estimate the jobs created and lost at new firms with a special birth-death model. Once a year, it finally has enough information to replace all those estimates with actual data for almost every job.

2. In the household survey, the BLS surveys 60,000 households across the country (barely 0.1 percent of the total) about their age, education, race, and whether they are working, and if not, why not. From that sample it estimates the unemployment rate, the participation rate, and the total number of people employed and unemployed for the whole country. Except for technical changes once a year these numbers are not revised.

Simply calling yourself unemployed is not enough to be counted as unemployed. The official definition is quite precise: You have to be available and have looked for work in the four weeks before the government takes its survey. You do not, however, have to be collecting unemployment insurance. In 2011, this official unemployment rate averaged 8.9 percent.

There are other ways of measuring unemployment:

- The U-4 unemployment rate includes the official unemployment rate plus discouraged workers: those who didn't look for work believing none was available. In 2011, it was 9.5 percent.
- The U-5 unemployment rate includes the U-4 measure plus any other "marginally-attached" workers: people who aren't looking for work but say they'd like a job. In 2011, it was 10.4 percent.
- The U-6 unemployment rate is the most popular expanded definition of unemployment. It includes the U-5 measure plus people working part time who would rather have a full-time job. In 2011, that figure was 15.9 percent.

There are many ways to measure the long-term unemployed but the most popular is those without work at least 27 weeks. In 2011, they represented 44 percent of the unemployed, compared to 18 percent in 2007.

If the payroll and household reports show employment going in opposite directions, you should usually trust the payroll survey.

The employment report can leave you scratching your head. For instance, you may hear that in one month employment fell, which is bad, but so did the unemployment rate, which is good. Why might this happen? There are two main reasons.

1. **Participation bounces around.** Some people counted as unemployed (and therefore part of the labor force) one month may not be the next, because they gave up looking for work, went back to school, or retired. When unemployment falls because of a drop in participation, it is usually a bad sign. Conversely, if unemployment rises because of higher participation, it is a good sign.

2. **Sometimes the two surveys diverge.** The payroll report may find fewer jobs while the household report finds more people employed. This can happen because employment surveys, like opinion polls, have margins of error, and different results are normal, statistical noise. Or it may result from the fact that the two surveys define employment differently. Someone working two jobs is counted twice in the payroll survey but just once in the household survey. Nannies, farm workers, and the self-employed are counted in the household survey but not in the payroll survey.

If the two surveys go in different directions, you should usually trust the payroll survey because its sample is much larger, and its job count is constantly revised as more complete information is received. But the payroll survey doesn't tell you anything about the unemployed or the characteristics of workers themselves. For that, you have to turn to the household survey. If the two reports show a persistent divergence in employment levels, it's a clue one is missing something important.

Another important job market indicator is the number of new claims that states receive for unemployment insurance. Because the U.S. Department of Labor reports total new claims each Thursday, this number is one of the earliest indicators of a shift in the health of the economy. The numbers are volatile, though. Holidays and bad weather can play havoc with the trend.

The Job Market of Tomorrow

In the 2000s, the natural rate of unemployment was probably around 5 percent. By 2012 the actual unemployment rate was 8 percent. Will we ever get back, or close, to that 5 percent rate? The path is strewn with obstacles.

First, as we learned in Chapter 3, recoveries after crises are sluggish. The lack of spending makes it harder for firms to ramp up sales and hire.

Second, many of the jobs lost in 2007 to 2009 are never coming back. In 1982, about 22 percent of the unemployed were on temporary layoff, and businesses called many back to work when sales recovered. In 2011, though, only 9 percent were on temporary layoff; for 40 percent of the unemployed, the jobs they lost were gone permanently. Another damper on job creation is that the longer someone is unemployed, the more their skills and habits waste away, making it harder to ever go back to work. Even when the economy has recovered, some of those people will struggle to find jobs.

The future structure of the workforce is changing as people tend to work later into their lives. For decades, a growing share of workers over the age of 55 retired before reaching 65; now, however, more are staying in the labor force. Incentives in Social Security and company pensions to retire early have now reversed, and people need to work longer to keep the lifestyle they want. It's also because work itself has changed. Someone who inhaled noxious vapors on a factory floor often couldn't work much past age 55, much less want to. But nowadays we teach or consult, we don't plough fields or mine coal, and we stay healthy longer. Not only can many Americans work longer, many want to.

As a result of these factors, the natural rate of unemployment, previously around 5 percent, is probably now around 6 percent.

The Bottom Line

- In the short run, the number of jobs rises and falls with the business cycle. In the long run, though, the growth in jobs usually tracks almost perfectly the growth in the number of people who want jobs.

- The unemployment rate is the single best signpost of the economy's health. When the economy reaches full strength, the unemployment reaches its so-called natural rate.

- Pay usually tracks productivity, which is why, over the years, workers have gotten richer. In recent decades, however, the best-paid workers have seen their salaries grow much more rapidly than the rest of the work force has, because of the premium on skills, weaker unions, and superstar salaries, whether for lawyers or for athletes.

Fire and Ice

———————— ∼ ————————

*Warning: Inflation and
Deflation Are Toxic to Your
Economic Health*

WHEN YUGOSLAVIA DISSOLVED INTO a bloody civil war in the 1990s, there were more than just ethnic and religious rivalries at work. Inflation, the continuous rise in the prices of almost everything, was also a factor. Thanks to an economic crisis in the early 1980s, prices in Yugoslavia were rising at annual rates of more than 1,200 percent by the late 1980s. Inflation helped

dissolve the cohesion of Yugoslavia's multiethnic middle class. Some people protected themselves by growing their own food or hoarding foreign currency. Others watched their incomes and savings get wiped out.

Throughout history, high inflation has often led to social upheaval. Hyperinflation, when prices rise by 50 percent or more per month, helped bring the Nazis to power in Germany and the communists in Russia and China, and topple both civilian and military governments in Argentina. These, of course, are extreme forms of the disease. But far more modest rates of inflation in the 1970s helped bring Margaret Thatcher to power in Britain in 1979 and drive Jimmy Carter from the White House.

Why is inflation so destabilizing?

Prices are the market's air supply; they signal surpluses and shortages and tell businesses and consumers when to produce more or consume less. Inflation contaminates this air supply. Suppose you are thinking of opening a new hotel in a city where room rates are rising 10 percent, thinking that must be a sign of strong demand. But what if the cost of land is going up 12 percent, linen by 11 percent, chambermaid and doormen wages by 13 percent? The new hotel may actually lose money. Inflation makes it hard to interpret price signals.

Inflation also unsettles people because it arbitrarily punishes some people while it rewards others. A retiree who buys a government bond that pays 4 percent interest, only to see inflation jump to 5 percent, sees his purchasing power get clobbered. A home buyer lucky enough to lock in a mortgage at 5 percent and then sees home prices soar 50 percent scores a windfall.

Inflation is also a hidden tax. As wages rise to compensate for it, so does tax revenue, making it easier for the government to repay what it borrowed before inflation took off. In the process, however, it robs the currency in people's wallets of purchasing power.

Another reason inflation is unsettling is that getting it back down is painful. Governments may resort to wage and price controls or other heavy-handed interventions to reduce inflation. Usually, though, it takes a recession to cure inflation—and that hurts everyone.

Goldman Sachs economists have shown that investors do best under low inflation (see Table 5.1). Under high inflation, only stocks gain, and not by much. Under hyperinflation, everything goes down.

Inflation's dangers should not be overstated. It is hard to find evidence that steady inflation below 5 percent does much economic harm. The trouble is that as inflation rises it gets less predictable. This year 5 percent, next year who knows?

Table 5.1 Investors Hate Inflation and Deflation

	Annual After-Inflation Returns		
	Cash	Bonds	Equities
Deflation			
United States, 1930–1933	7.3	10.7	−6.2
Japan, 1998–2003	0.4	2.3	0.7
Problem inflation			
United States, 1967–1980	−6.4	−3.1	1.1
Turkey, 1971–2002	−33.4	0.8	2.7
Hyperinflation			
Germany, 1922–1923	−100.0	−100.0	−100.0
Brazil, 1988–1993	−93.3		−67.3

Source: Goldman Sachs Global Economics Paper #190, September 2009.

From Cigarettes to Aztecs

There are two competing schools of thought on the cause of inflation, and listening to their proponents is like listening to creationists and Darwinians argue over how life began. The monetarist school blames the *money supply*, while the New Keynesian school blames a combination of *excess spending* and *inflationary psychology*.

Blame It on the Money Supply

Milton Friedman, the Nobel economist, said "Inflation is always and everywhere a monetary phenomenon." *Monetarism*, as this brand of economics is called, blames

inflation on too much money chasing too few goods. Intuitively, this makes sense. If you double the amount of money people spend on stuff, but leave unchanged the amount of stuff, prices will double.

~

There are two competing schools of thought on the cause of inflation. Listening to them is like listening to creationists and Darwinians argue over how life began.

In its most basic form, this notion is uncontroversial, and economists of all stripes accept it. Let's examine one example. In German prisoner-of-war camps, prisoners used cigarettes as currency, pricing bread, shirts, and chocolates in cigarettes. When Red Cross shipments arrived, suddenly everyone had more cigarettes to spend—and the prices of everything went up. As the cigarettes wore out or were smoked, prices started dropping again. Altering the supply of money has the same effect. When the government finances its spending with taxes or by borrowing, the money comes from taxpayers and savers. But if it finances its spending

by printing money, or more precisely, by issuing bonds to the central bank, the money is created out of thin air. With all that extra money chasing the same goods and services, prices rise. In the extreme this can produce *hyperinflation*, when prices rise 50 percent or more *per month*. In 2008 in Zimbabwe, prices were doubling roughly every day. Steven Hanke, a Johns Hopkins University economist, figures annual inflation equaled 89.7 sextillion percent (that's 897 followed by 20 zeros). During such hyperinflations, people try to hold as little currency as possible. As soon as they're paid, they spend the money before its value is wiped out. In many cases, people switch to foreign currency instead.

At the opposite extreme, fixing the money supply eradicates persistent inflation. That's what happens when a country goes on the *gold standard* under which currency and bank deposits can be converted, at a fixed rate, to gold. This did not guarantee stable prices. In normal times, banks might issue $10 worth of currency and deposits for each dollar of gold they actually held, and use that to make $10 of loans. In boom times when confidence was running high, they might issue $12. This boosted the money supply and prices. But eventually people would demand their gold back. To redeem currency and deposits, banks would have to call in loans. Credit would contract and prices fall. When the

United States was on the gold standard between 1790 and 1911, inflation and deflation alternated; wholesale prices ended the period roughly where they began.

Under some conditions, though, the money supply can rise even with a gold standard in place. How? The supply of gold may increase. For example, when Spanish conquerors brought troves of Aztec and Inca treasures back to Europe, a century of mild inflation ensued. Or, another way this can happen is if the government allows the same amount of gold to back a larger amount of currency. Roman emperors and medieval kings routinely debased their coins—that is, they reduced their gold or silver content—to finance their wars. From 1933 to 1934, Franklin D. Roosevelt allowed gold to rise from $20.67 to $35 per troy ounce, a 41 percent devaluation, in a successful effort to end deflation.

Thus far, the link between the money supply and inflation is straightforward. It's when you get to the case of a modern economy that monetarism proves almost useless in practice. Let's examine why.

The central bank doesn't control the entire money supply, only a narrow portion of it: specifically, the notes, coins, and reserves it supplies to commercial banks. (*Reserves* are cash that banks keep on deposit at the Fed to settle payments with each other, with the Treasury, or to exchange for currency to refill their ATMs.)

To understand why the link between money supply and inflation is muddy, imagine that the Fed distributes $1 trillion in freshly printed 20-dollar bills to people on street corners. If they promptly rush home and stuff the money under their mattresses, what will happen to consumer spending and inflation? Zilch. For money to cause inflation, it must be lent and spent. Banks lend when they have healthy balance sheets and a lot of eager, creditworthy customers. Consumers spend when they feel confident about their jobs and salaries; they go to the ATM more often, run up bigger credit card bills, remodel their homes, and buy faster cars.

Monetarists claim that growth in the money supply leads to more spending and more inflation. Actually, it's the other way around. Every dollar consumers borrow or spend returns to the banking system and shows up in someone else's checking or savings deposit or money market mutual fund, which are all part of the broader money supply (which has labels like M1, M2, and M3).

For this reason, the Fed doesn't target the money supply. It normally uses its control of reserves only to ensure banks have enough cash to keep their ATMs full, and to control short-term interest rates. (In Chapter 11 I explain how it does this and why it has deviated from that practice in recent years.) Therefore,

its influence over the broad money supply is indirect. If it raises interest rates, it will dampen spending and, eventually, the money supply. If, however, the economy is truly moribund, because no one wants to lend or borrow, the Fed can drive interest rates to zero and print gobs of money without causing broader measures of money and credit to grow. That's what happened between the fall of 2008 and early 2011: The Fed lowered rates to almost zero and "printed" $1.5 trillion (in the form of currency and new bank reserves), yet total bank lending contracted.

The Other Side of the Story: Mind the Gap and Your Mind

So don't preoccupy yourself with the money supply. For a more realistic picture of inflation—the new-Keynesian picture—think instead of hotels in Scottsdale, Arizona. The supply of rooms is roughly the same all year, but there's a lot more demand in January when the temperature averages 70 degrees than in July when it averages 100 degrees. Because the demand for rooms is higher in January, the hotel can charge a lot more than in July.

The same is true for the economy as a whole: When the demand for all goods and services runs ahead of the supply (i.e., potential output), inflation rises. When demand falls short of potential, inflation falls.

When unemployment is below its natural rate, workers are better able to win raises. This relationship was captured by Alban William Phillips, a New Zealand economist. The Phillips Curve, which shows an inverse relationship between unemployment and inflation, is at the heart of the new Keynesian inflation model.

A hotel whose occupancy suddenly rises to 95 percent from 80 percent will eventually add rooms, but will first simply charge more. Similarly, if occupancy falls, the hotel may eventually close. But first, it will simply charge less. The difference between actual gross domestic product (GDP) and potential GDP is the output gap, which you could think of as a vacancy rate for the entire economy. Inflation always falls after recessions because the output gap is so large: Hotels and office buildings are empty, factories are idle, and the unemployed are everywhere.

~

Inflation needs a wage-price spiral; if wages don't rise, there's no spiral.

Like the natural rate of unemployment, potential output is a slippery thing to measure. It's easy to tell if a hotel, factory, or power plant is at full capacity. But what

about a law firm or an Internet dating service? Potential also changes. In the early 1970s, high oil prices rendered a lot of existing factories obsolete; this reduced potential. In the late 1990s, companies found they could use the computers and the Internet to boost production with fewer workers. For example, airlines replaced reservation agents with websites. This boosted potential.

Finally, potential is affected by actual economic activity. Between 1997 and 2001, official estimates of America's long-term potential were revised up by 12 percent because the tech boom had spurred investment and innovation and encouraged lots of people to join the labor force. The 2007 to 2009 bust did the opposite, reducing estimated potential by 5 percent. It is difficult to know when the economy has exceeded its capacity, but there are telltale signs. The surest sign is if firms are paying higher wages to attract qualified workers. Wages and benefits represent 55 percent of all the costs of production; if they rise persistently, that must ultimately be passed on to prices. If wages don't rise, a wage-price spiral can't happen.

An economy with a large output gap can grow rapidly with little threat of inflation, just as an empty hotel won't raise room rates just because a few guests checked in. But once the output gap has been closed, the

economy can only grow in line with the labor force and productivity. For the United States, that means a growth rate between 2.25 and 2.75 percent.

Strange as it may seem, inflation also depends a lot on what people *think* it will be. Suppose an employer and its union sit down to hammer out a new contract. If both parties agree inflation will be 2 percent, they will quickly agree to a 2 percent cost-of-living increase and the firm will plan on setting prices to cover those costs. If every firm in the country and its employees do the same thing, inflation will settle at 2 percent. Thus, expectations of inflation can be self-fulfilling.

Rapidly shifting expectations lead to quicker changes in inflation. If a jump in oil prices suddenly boosts the cost of living, firms and workers quickly raise wages and prices to compensate, and a wage-price spiral ensues. This means that the trade-off between inflation and unemployment in the Phillips Curve is only temporary. Pushing the economy past its potential can drive down unemployment for a little while, but as inflation picks up, so will workers' wage demands, and unemployment will drop back to where it was.

On the other hand, if people have gotten used to 2 percent inflation year in and year out, they might endure a jump in oil prices without expecting wages to automatically follow. Well-anchored expectations can keep

inflation steady even when the economy is above or below potential.

Even Worse than Inflation

Inflation is a familiar scourge. *Deflation*, when prices are falling, is rarer and, potentially, nastier. This may seem odd. Shouldn't we be happy if the prices we pay go down year after year? Well, it's sort of like weight loss. What's the reason for it: You're eating better and exercising more (good), or starving to death (bad)?

Good deflation occurs when workers and companies become more productive and learn to make things at a lower cost. Intel, for example, is continuously cutting the price of computer chips because it keeps finding new, cheaper ways to make them. Intel's profits and its employees' salaries still go up. If you multiply that across the entire economy, it's possible for prices to fall across the board even as incomes rise.

Bad deflation occurs when spending collapses and companies have to cut their prices to prop up sales, just as hotels cut their rates when tourist traffic dries up. If people expect falling prices, they may delay purchases since their money will buy more later. Workers initially resist pay cuts, so employers must lay some off to cope with falling prices. Eventually, fear of unemployment persuades workers to accept lower pay. Prices and wages

follow each other down, the mirror image of an infla-
tionary wage-price spiral. We saw this happen between
1929 and 1933 in the United States when prices fell 7
percent per year. Japan has endured a milder form of
this bad deflation since the late 1990s.

If prices and wages are falling at the same rate, is
anyone the worse for it? Paychecks have shrunk but
because prices have as well, purchasing power remains
the same. The problem is that debt is fixed so as incomes
and prices fall, the burden of debt rises. Homeowners
slash spending to keep up with their mortgage pay-
ments. Or worse, the homeowner goes into foreclosure
because he or she is "underwater": The home can't be
sold for enough to repay the loan. The bank fails, deep-
ening the economic stress. "The more the economic
boat tips, the more it tends to tip," wrote Irving Fisher,
the American economist who labeled this phenomenon
debt-deflation in 1933.

Deflation can be harder to cure than inflation. Faced
with inflation, a central bank can generally raise interest
rates as high as it wants. Faced with recession, it can
stimulate spending and restore growth by lowering its
interest rate below the inflation rate, making the *real*
cost of borrowing *negative*. Clearly, that's impossible
when inflation itself is negative, because the central
bank can't lower interest rates below zero: During

deflation the *real* interest rate will always be positive. (In Chapter 11, I describe other tools the central bank can use if it's already lowered short-term rates to zero.)

The People's Choice

In the wake of the Great Recession, monetarists looked at the ballooning money supply and warned of inflation. New Keynesians looked at the gigantic output gap and warned of deflation. The schizophrenia was nicely encapsulated in a country-and-western YouTube ditty by Merle Hazard, the pseudonym of Jon Shayne, a money manager:

> Inflation or deflation, tell me if you can:
> will we become Zimbabwe or will we be Japan?

**In the long run, inflation
is a political choice.**

Neither happened. Inflation lurched up and down with gyrating oil prices but the underlying rate stayed near 2 percent, where it stood before the recession. Costlier oil worked its way into all sorts of prices, but

high unemployment kept a lid on wages. People continued to expect inflation of around 2 to 3 percent, which has made it hard for either inflation or deflation to get a toehold.

What does the future hold? In the short run, economic factors like the output gap, oil prices and expectations drive inflation. But in the long run, politics dominate: Voters and governments choose the inflation they want through the goals and leaders they give to their central banks.

Higher inflation is especially tempting now. By making real interest rates even more negative, it could stimulate borrowing, spending, and employment. It would boost prices, wages, and tax revenue, making it easier for companies, workers, and governments to repay their crushing debts, though this would hurt savers. Tempting as this may sound, it's politically treacherous: Voters hate inflation. In two centuries, the United States has experienced only one peacetime episode of severe inflation: It rose from 3 percent in 1966 to nearly 14 percent in 1980. By that point, people consistently rated inflation a bigger concern than unemployment in Gallup polls. More recently, Republicans in Congress have attacked the Federal Reserve for trying to kick start economic growth by expanding the money supply via "quantitative easing" (discussed in Chapter 11), and

would like the law changed to reinforce the Fed's responsibility for keeping inflation down. Conversely, the absence of political retribution can make deflation hard to eradicate: Many Japanese, especially retirees on fixed incomes, like deflation.

Into the Weeds

When the Bureau of Labor Statistics (BLS) was created in the late nineteenth century, the cost of living was one of the first things it tried to measure. Today, the consumer price index (CPI) is the economic statistic that most affects Americans' daily lives because it is used to calculate cost-of-living adjustments. Once a month, BLS statisticians and contractors fan out across the country and visit thousands of businesses to collect prices on more than 80,000 items in 200 categories from new cars to funerals. It uses regular surveys of consumers' spending habits to assign a weight to each category in the index—32 percent for shelter, 0.3 percent for sugar and candy. The 12-month percentage change in the CPI is the most common measure of inflation.

Fresh food and energy account for many of the monthly swings in the CPI. Because an increase one month is often undone a few months later, economists regularly exclude food and energy. The remainder, or

core inflation, provides a more stable picture of underlying inflation. This picture will be misleading, though, if energy and food costs march steadily higher (or lower) over time instead of reverting to their old levels.

The CPI isn't flawless. Consumers are constantly shifting to stores that have cheaper prices—to Walmart, for example, from pricey department stores, and to cheaper products, such as Internet telephone calls instead of landline calls. The CPI tries to capture these changes by surveying consumers' spending habits every two years, but in between, it may slightly overstate inflation.

There are other inflation measures, including:

- **PCE index**. An important but little-known alternative to the CPI is the price index of personal consumption expenditures, or PCE index, which the Bureau of Economic Analysis uses to calculate GDP. The Federal Reserve's forecasts are based on the PCE index rather than the CPI. The PCE is based on what businesses actually sell rather than what consumers say they buy (which may be flawed). As a result, it assigns less importance to housing than the CPI, and more to medical care. The PCE index has quirks, too—it puts a price on things that have no price, like Sunday mass and no-fee checking accounts.

- **GDP deflator.** The GDP deflator measures prices paid by all sectors of the economy: businesses, government, foreign buyers of exports, as well as consumers. It's used to calculate how much of an increase in nominal GDP is due to inflation and how much is real activity.
- **Producer price index.** The producer price index (PPI) measures the prices that sellers receive, rather than what consumers pay. Because the main PPI excludes services, it is a much narrower measure of inflation than the CPI, and it is much more volatile.

~

Gold and commodity prices are much better measures of the fear of inflation than predictors of inflation.

- **Inflation expectations.** These expectations can be monitored through surveys. Each month, the Thomson Reuters/University of Michigan Surveys of Consumers asks consumers what they expect inflation to be over the next year, and the next 5 to 10 years. Treasury inflation-protected

securities (TIPS) provide a minute-by-minute measure of investors' inflation expectations. If a TIPS bond yields 3 percent and a regular bond yields 5 percent, the difference, 2 percent, is the expected inflation rate. Be cautious with this because technical factors having nothing to do with inflation push these yields around.

- **Gold and commodity prices.** Many investors look to gold and commodity prices for early warning signs of inflation and deflation. These prices are much better measures of the fear of inflation than predictors of inflation. That's partly because so many other things affect them. Gold responds to global unrest, the demand for jewelry, and the dollar. Commodity prices respond to the strength of the global economy, strikes, and bad weather.

- **Wages and labor costs.** Hourly and weekly wages can be tracked each month in the BLS's payroll survey that I discussed in Chapter 4. The quarterly employment cost index is more comprehensive because it also includes benefits and bonuses. Benefits for health care, pensions, and payroll taxes are now almost 20 percent of compensation, up from 5 percent in the 1940s. Still, to determine if rising wages are inflationary, you have to compare them to productivity.

If a painter's salary doubles because he can now paint twice as much with a paint sprayer, his salary per square foot has not risen at all. Labor costs, adjusted for productivity, are measured through unit labor costs, which the BLS reports quarterly along with productivity.

The Bottom Line

- High inflation is destabilizing and corrosive; deflation can be destructive. The best inflation is not too high nor too low: from 1 to 3 percent seems about right.

- The money supply is a lousy guide to where inflation is going. Better, instead, to monitor how far the economy is operating from its capacity. For example, if unemployment is 5 percent, it doesn't have much spare capacity left. Wages are the best evidence of an economy running out of capacity. If wages aren't rising, a wage-price spiral can't happen.

- Inflation is more likely to rise if people expect it to, because they'll adjust their wage and price behavior accordingly. Stable inflation expectations are a bulwark against both inflation and deflation.

Chapter Six

Drop the Puck!

~

The Globalization Game Is Here Whether We're Ready or Not

In the summer of 2006, Israel fought a fierce, one-month war with Hezbollah. Israeli jets pounded southern Lebanon while Hezbollah rained rockets on northern Israel, sending residents into bomb shelters and emptying the beaches, stores, and port of Haifa, one of Israel's largest cities. Yet Israel's stock market was higher when the war was over than when it began.

That year Israel's economy grew 5 percent and its currency soared.

Why so little harm to the country's economy amidst so much destructive violence? In a word: *globalization*. Israel's economy is led by advanced technology companies whose markets are the rest of the world. Just before the war, Warren Buffett acquired Iscar Metalworking Company, a precision metal-cutting tool maker. It was hit by a rocket but never missed a shipment. During the war, Hewlett Packard made one of the largest ever acquisitions of a predominantly Israeli high-tech company.

Globalization is the increased flow of goods, services, people, ideas, and capital across borders. As economies merge with each other, interest rates in one country respond to the whims of investors an ocean away, local companies' sales depend on the tastes of foreign consumers, and local consumers can choose from a cornucopia of foreign and domestic offerings. As such, globalization means more is riding on the skills of a country's own citizens. If they produce something the world wants, their ability to serve a far larger market translates into higher productivity and salaries. It also leaves a country at the mercy of the rest of the world's health. Israel didn't have a banking crisis but because its major trading partners did, it followed them into recession in 2009.

A Gravitational Pull from Afar

When you study economic growth, jobs, and interest rates you have to keep in mind that globalization is exerting an often hidden influence, the way a distant planet's gravitational pull alters another planet's orbit. A perfect example came in mid-2011 when the price of gold soared above $1,500 per ounce. Since people often buy gold when they worry that paper currencies will lose their value, many commentators saw it as proof that Federal Reserve policies were about to send inflation in the United States skyrocketing. They were right about inflation but wrong about the country. The real problem was in China and India, which together buy more than half the world's gold. In both, rising inflation in early 2011 helped propel a surge in gold buying.

The best yardstick of this growing interdependence is in the remarkable expansion of global trade. Since 1950, growth in global trade has outstripped that of world gross domestic product (GDP) growth by 6 percent to 4 percent, according to the World Trade Organization (WTO). Exports account for more than 40 percent of China's, Germany's and Israel's GDP, and more than 80 percent of Ireland's.

Exports were traditionally less important to the United States because its own internal market was so

huge. That's less true now: exports rose from 5 percent of GDP in the 1960s to 14 percent in 2012. As many once-poor countries join the ranks of the affluent, their appetite for imports grows, and they become a more enticing market for American companies. In 2000, so-called emerging markets represented 20 percent of world GDP (measured in dollars). By 2012, they were 38 percent.

We usually think the benefit of international trade is more exports. But that's a blinkered view. Imports are just as important, perhaps more important, because they enrich consumers. Think of all the things you'd forsake if borders were closed: fresh fruit and tropical flowers in the dead of winter, British novelist J. K. Rowling's Harry Potter novels, cheap oil from Saudi Arabia (okay, a mixed blessing), Hyundais.

Countries even benefit by importing something they could make themselves. Why do parents hire a nanny when they could stay home and raise their child themselves? Because it lets them earn enough money to buy a nicer home and send the child to college. The same principle of *comparative advantage* is why rich countries buy toys and clothing from poor countries: so that their own workers can earn more building aircraft, conducting heart bypass operations, or making movies. Yet, comparative advantage doesn't explain why many countries export and import similar things. For example, why

does France sells Renaults to Germany while Germany exports Volkswagens to France? Because consumers like choice. Just as your town has numerous pizzerias catering to different tastes in pizza, French and German consumers want to choose from more than just a few brands of car.

Giving consumers this much choice would be impossible without globalization. Unlike pizzas, cars require huge economies of scale to make cheaply and a single country's market by itself can't support more than a few brands. When global barriers come down, numerous small national markets become a big global market that numerous companies can now profitably serve. Singapore and Luxembourg are tiny countries but are among the richest because their companies and consumers are part of a global market. The competition inevitably improves the quality of the domestic product, such as when a flood of Japanese imported cars forced U.S. manufacturers to improve their own quality.

It's Complicated

To economists, the benefits of both exports and imports are so obvious that it's one of the few things this notoriously fractious profession agrees on. Yet, in recent years, trade has changed radically, rattling even normally stalwart supporters. Traditionally, we bought toys,

clothing, and other things from poor countries that required more manual and less intellectual labor. We bought more advanced products like aircraft, software, and microprocessor chips from other rich countries.

But in recent decades, China, India, and Russia have joined the global workforce and now sell the sorts of advanced products we long thought were invulnerable to such competition. The collapsing cost of blasting megabytes of data across undersea cables makes it possible for foreigners to read Americans' X-rays, take their hotel reservations, or report on town council meetings. Alan Blinder, a former vice-chairman of the Federal Reserve, has estimated that perhaps a quarter of U.S. jobs can now be done offshore.

~

The expansion of trade from things we drop on our foot to things we carry around in our brains terrifies many Americans.

This expansion of trade from things we drop on our foot to things we carry around in our brains terrifies many Americans who fear that even the most advanced jobs will disappear at the hands of foreign competition. Just consider the storm of criticism that greeted Greg

Mankiw, a Harvard professor who, while serving as chairman of George Bush's Council of Economic Advisers in 2004, said outsourcing was just as beneficial as traditional trade. The Republican Speaker of the House, Dennis Hastert, accused Mankiw of failing a "basic test of real economics."

But, Mankiw was right. Although cheaply written software from India may put some U.S. programmers out of work, it makes U.S. consumers of software better off. Cheap software may help some U.S. companies develop products that they can then sell abroad. This then enables the company to hire the laid-off programmers in a new capacity. A study by Ashish Arora, Lee Branstetter, and Matej Drev argues that the American technology industry recaptured the lead from Japan's in the 1990s by tapping cheap foreign talent either in India, or working in the United States on temporary visas, for routine software programming. This freed up their more innovative engineers to work on transformative projects, raising their productivity.

That so many Americans are fearful of outsourcing is understandable. Why, they might imagine, would anyone pay them (or a Japanese or British worker) more than a Chinese or Indian worker with the same university degree? The reason is that a U.S. worker's productivity comes not just from her own education and skill

but the social, economic, and political infrastructure around her: The advanced equipment she uses, the cables that transmit her telephone, and Internet traffic free of static and brownouts across the country and back, highways that get her and her coworkers to the office and their products to market, trustworthy courts that enforce contracts and settle disputes with customers and suppliers.

~

Although trade does not rob Americans of jobs, it alters the balance between winners and losers.

The United States is especially strong at exporting products with a lot of intellectual content. Services such as music and films make up roughly a third of its exports. The three tallest skyscrapers on Shanghai's skyline, the Jin Mao Tower, the Shanghai World Financial Center, and the Shanghai Tower (to be completed in 2015) were all designed by American architectural firms and structural engineers.

Apple employs just 43,000 people in the United States but more than 10 times that many through

contractors in other countries, in particular China.* But because its Chinese workers are paid so much less, they contribute far less of the value to Apple's products than the Americans who design and market them. According to a study by the Personal Computing Industry Centre at the University of California, Irvine, just 2 percent of all the wages earned in the sale of an iPod are earned in China, while 70 percent are earned in the United States. When Apple sells an iPod in Germany, it shows up as an export from China, but most of the benefit flows back to the United States.

If Apple made all its products in the United States, the higher wages paid to American workers would make the products much more expensive and fewer people would buy them. This, then, illustrates something important: Trade with China, or any poor country, does not make Americans collectively poorer; it does alter *the balance between winners and losers*. In the case of the iPod, the winners are buyers of iPods, Apple's executives and shareholders, and its other employees. The losers are the people who may have assembled iPods in the United States but can't compete with Chinese wages. Trade can thus aggravate inequality, eroding wages for formerly middle-class workers while rewarding those at the top.

*New York Times, January 21, 2012.

A Question of Balances: Trade Deficits and Surpluses

Trade has expanded over time because affluent consumers want more choice, transport costs have plummeted (to zero, for digital products), and barriers to trade have fallen.

Even as exports and imports grow over time, though, countries may swing from a trade surplus—that is, from exporting more than it imports—to a trade deficit and back, because of short-term influences, including:

- **How healthy a country and its trading partners are.** If European consumers are sickly and U.S. consumers are robust, the United States will import a lot from Europe but its exports to Europe will suffer, which will widen the U.S. trade deficit.

- **Export and import prices.** If you own an apartment in a neighborhood that suddenly becomes fashionable, you can raise the rent without investing a dime on renovations. Similarly, a country blessed with resources the rest of the world wants reaps a windfall. Russia's trade surplus soared in the 2000s because soaring demand made its oil

more valuable. The reverse is also true. Like a tenant whose rent doubles because his neighborhood has gentrified, the United States had to pay more for oil in the 2000s because it was so much in demand by other countries.

• **Exchange rate.** A lower currency makes exports cheaper and imports more expensive, so shifts in the exchange rate have a big impact on trade deficits and surpluses. But the impact may be fleeting, for reasons I discuss in Chapter 8.

≈

Some countries run deficits year after year while others run surpluses. This reflects different saving and spending habits.

These factors can push exports and imports up or down in the short run yet some countries run deficits year after year while others run surpluses. Such persistent gaps reflect underlying differences in spending and saving. The United States persistently consumes and invests more than it produces because it has a shortage of saving. That extra consumption thus sucks in imports, leading to a trade deficit. Conversely, a country

that always consumes less than it produces will have a trade surplus. Germany has chronically weak consumer spending, a reflection of its aging population and a national obsession with saving. German stores don't open on Sunday unless they're in railway or gas stations and can only have sales on certain days of the year.

Meet Mr. Smoot and Mr. Hawley

Global trade is one of the great economic success stories. One study by Scott Bradford, Paul Grieco, and Gary Hufbauer estimates the average U. S. household is some $10,000 per year richer thanks to the postwar expansion of trade.

Given that, you'd think tearing down tariffs, quotas, and other barriers to trade would be wildly popular. In fact, the public and politicians generally prefer protectionism—that is, the sheltering of domestic industries from foreign competition—to free trade.

Free trade is a tough sell because its benefits are less obvious than its costs. Imports make the majority of consumers better off, but they seldom know or care, whereas companies and workers that lose their livelihoods to imports are quick to let their representatives in Congress know. Given this political hostility, it's remarkable that free trade has made so much progress.

In 1930 Herbert Hoover signed into law the Smoot-Hawley Tariff Act. It raised tariffs on thousands of products and triggered outrage and, in some cases, retaliation from other countries. Global trade was already collapsing, but Smoot-Hawley accelerated the process.

Fear of a repeat has since helped free trade put down roots in the halls of power around the world. In 1934, the Reciprocal Trade Agreements Act shifted responsibility for trade policy to the president who is less susceptible to narrow, protectionist interests and more likely to see trade agreements as a foreign policy bargaining chip. In 1947, the world signed onto global rules under the General Agreement on Tariffs and Trade (GATT). In 1995, GATT changed its name to the World Trade Organization (WTO). Visitors often ask the WTO's chief, Pascal Lamy, if the two men whose pictures hang in his office are his relatives. He says they are Senator Reed Smoot and Representative Willis Hawley, the "true founders" of the WTO.

Signatories to the WTO abide by common rules on the treatment of each other's exports and imports, curbing protectionism.

Still, like a virus, protectionism is always mutating, from the tariffs, quotas, and subsidies of old to preferential government procurement ("Buy American" or

"Buy Chinese"), restrictive licensing requirements, local monopolies, and trumped-up health, safety, and environmental standards. The United States kept Mexican truckers off its roads for 17 years after the passage of the North American Free Trade Agreement (NAFTA), claiming Mexican drivers are not safe, when in reality U.S. truckers just didn't want the competition.

One way countries have sought to protect themselves is by joining bilateral and regional trade groups, like the European Union and NAFTA. The United States has signed free trade agreements with 18 different countries. China is busy signing trade agreements. While such pacts boost trade between the signatories, they siphon support for global efforts to reduce barriers, and over time may weaken the WTO.

Into the Weeds

The benefits of trade are a matter of high-minded economics, but trade relations are a bare-knuckle business. The president conducts trade policy through the U.S. trade representative. The trade representative is not there to debate the nuances of economic theory but to cajole and threaten other countries. The House of Representatives' Committee on Ways and Means and the Senate Finance Committee oversee trade policy. The Senate must ratify treaties. Other countries are

reluctant to sign a treaty that the Congress may amend before ratifying. To smooth the way, Congress sometimes gives the president *trade promotion authority* (also called *Fast Track*), which permits him to negotiate treaties that Congress can approve or reject, but not amend.

Individual legislators regularly try to take trade into their own hands. Dozens of bills, for example, in recent years aimed to hit China for keeping its currency artificially low. None have become law, but both George W. Bush and Barack Obama used them as leverage to get China to let its currency rise.

Complaints about imports usually fall into one of three categories. A *subsidy* is a government grant or some other favorable treatment that lowers the cost of the import. *Dumping* occurs when a foreign company sells its products abroad for less than it costs to make them, or for less than it charges at home. A *surge* is a sudden increase in imports.

Subsidy and dumping complaints are heard by the Import Administration, part of the Commerce Department. If the Import Administration agrees subsidies or dumping have occurred, as it does 95 percent of the time, it sends the complaint to the federal International Trade Commission (ITC), an independent, bipartisan panel, to determine if the subsidy or dumping actually hurt anyone in the United States.

About 60 percent of the time it concludes that it did. In the case of subsidy it recommends a countervailing duty. In the case of dumping it recommends an antidumping duty. The president has little discretion here: If the ITC says injury has occurred, the Commerce Department generally has to impose the duty.

Like a hockey referee, the WTO gives countries an impartial venue to settle their trade disputes rather than mixing it up in the parking lot.

A company accused of causing a surge of imports hasn't actually done anything wrong: It's just making it hard for local competitors to survive. U.S. companies or unions can ask for a safeguard against the surge under one of two laws: Section 201, which applies to any country, or Section 421, which only applies to China. Safeguard cases are decided by the ITC. If it concludes that a safeguard is warranted, the president has the discretion to say no.

World trade is like hockey: Fights are inevitable, but they're more dangerous when the players leave the rink and settle matters in the parking lot. Like the referee who hands out the penalties and lets the game continue, the WTO gives countries an impartial venue to settle their trade disputes rather than mixing it up in the parking lot. In 2002, George W. Bush slapped tariffs on steel from numerous countries. Rather than strike back, the European Union complained to the WTO. The WTO ruled the tariffs illegal and gave the EU permission to retaliate. As the EU drew up a list of retaliatory moves, Bush backed down, and withdrew the tariffs. The EU declared victory and sheathed its sword.

Still, free trade is a tough sell at the best times, and won't make much progress in coming years, if any. Prolonged high unemployment only makes people and their leaders more suspicious of competition. The global balance of power is also changing. For decades the United States let China and other poor countries get away with protectionism in the interests of letting them catch up. China is still poor but Americans now see it as a full-fledged economic and political rival and expect it to play by rich-country rules.

The Bottom Line

- Falling trade barriers, rising affluence, and the plunging cost of selling things across borders have fueled globalization. Able to buy from and sell to the entire world, even small countries can achieve exceptional levels of wealth.

- Trade makes the United States as a whole richer. But the benefits are not shared equally. Especially as services trade grows, the biggest gainers will be the highest skilled workers while those with the least skills will see their wages erode.

- Free trade is politically unpopular and every country routinely indulges its protectionist impulses. Yet free trade survives because countries have also agreed to subject their actions to the rules of the World Trade Organization, which keeps trade spats from becoming trade wars.

All the World's an ATM

~

*Knitting Global
Markets Together*

THE MESS CREATED by subprime mortgages issued to people of doubtful credit should have been the United States' private headache. After all, the loans were dreamed up to satisfy the American obsession with homeownership. Yet, to leverage themselves to the hilt, Americans had to borrow. If they could only borrow from other Americans, the competition for money would have driven up U.S. interest rates and snuffed out the frenzy.

But, as we learned in the previous chapter, economic borders are melting, in particular for borrowers. Factory workers in Shanghai, mutual fund investors in the United States, sovereign wealth funds in the Persian Gulf, and banks in Düsseldorf are all connected to a global ATM that continuously channels money from savers in one part of the world to borrowers in another. Thus, when U.S. homeowners and the U.S. Treasury needed money, the global ATM matched them to Germans, Chinese, and Saudis who needed a place to invest their savings.

When home prices turned down, the pain was felt not just in the U.S. financial system but by the banks and investors of every country that helped finance the housing boom. IKB, a once sleepy German bank that ran out of opportunities to lend to local businesses, loaded up on subprime mortgage-backed securities. In 2007, it had to be bailed out by the German government. It was joined in the injured ward by French, Swiss, and British banks, Australian hedge funds, and Norwegian municipalities.

The subprime mortgage crisis eloquently demonstrates how the global markets for assets, debts, and currencies have knit the world together. It provides many benefits, such as helping countries finance investment when they don't have enough savings and enabling

investors and borrowers alike to spread their risks around. But just as modern jet travel allows viruses to cross oceans, modern capital markets rapidly transmit one country's problems to others. And unlike with trade, the currency and capital markets aren't governed by shared rules of the road. They're a free-for-all prone to crisis.

Financing Deficits and More

If you spend more than you earn, you cover the difference by running up your credit card, running down your savings, or cashing in some investments. For a country, the equivalent is running a *current account deficit*—paying foreigners more for imports, interest, and dividends than it receives from them. To finance such a deficit, a country has to either borrow or sell some assets, such as stocks, bonds, Rockefeller Center, or a beer company to foreigners, with the result that the country's foreign debt mounts.

There's nothing wrong with a current account deficit. Just as a start-up company needs outside investors to develop its technology, a country often lacks the savings to exploit its bountiful investment opportunities. Foreigners lend it money or purchase shares in its companies so that it can build railroads, dig mines, or erect factories. The investments make the country wealthier,

generating wages and profits to repay the foreign investor.

Nowadays, though, far more capital crosses borders than what's needed simply to finance deficits. In 2011, for example, foreigners bought and sold about $60 trillion worth of U.S. stocks and bonds, more than 12 times total imports and exports that year. According to the Bank for International Settlements, foreign exchange trading now averages $4 trillion *per day*. These flows do more than transfer money from a saver in one country to a borrower in another; they make it possible for both investors and borrowers to diversify. U.S. investors, for instance, can diversify their portfolios by owning mature, stable U.S. companies and riskier but faster growing companies from Brazil and China, while U.S. companies can finance their expansion by raising money from Brazilian hedge funds and Chinese banks.

Still, the stunning scale of capital movements poses huge risks. Imagine carrying a cookie sheet filled with water across the kitchen floor. Just the slightest trip and water sloshes over the sides. The global capital market is like that cookie sheet. Enormous amounts of money flow effortlessly across borders around the clock but even a minor disturbance can divert huge sums from one market to another, sending stocks, interest rates, and currencies sharply up or down.

~
Major financial crises usually involve excessive borrowing from abroad.

The easy availability of global capital means a country can finance bigger deficits for longer than when capital was less mobile and harder to get. Most of the time that's good, but sometimes it lets a country dig itself deeper into debt. Major financial crises usually involve excessive borrowing from abroad. In the 1970s, western banks enthusiastically lent billions to Latin America. In the early 1980s, many of those countries couldn't pay the money back, seriously wounding many American banks. The Asian financial crisis began in 1997 when investors fled countries they feared could not repay loans taken out in foreign currencies. In the late 1990s, the United States ran current account deficits reflecting its companies' hunger for capital to invest in new technology. In the 2000s, it kept on running current account deficits, but this time to finance our lifestyles, such as suburban McMansions with granite-topped kitchen counters. They did nothing to enhance future growth.

In the next chapter, we'll discuss an even more devastating example of a borrowing binge that ended badly: the euro-zone crisis.

The American Dollar: The World's Problem

One of the rewards for the United States for emerging as the economic superpower after World War II was that its dollar became the place where global central banks liked to park their spare cash. At the end of 2011, the world's central banks held $11 trillion in reserves between them and 60 percent were in dollars, insofar as could be determined.

The U.S. Treasury bond market is to the world what money market mutual funds are to ordinary investors: a safe, dull place to store cash you need in a hurry.

The dollar owes its reserve-currency status first to the United States' leading share of the global economy. Most countries in the world do business with the United States. International trade is routinely priced in dollars even when an American isn't in on the transaction. The United States' legal and political stability means anyone with dollars is pretty sure the country that printed them will still exist when the time comes to spend them.

The dollar will lose this status one day as the United States' share of global GDP shrinks. But for now there are no realistic rivals. Because of China's capital controls, the yuan is mostly useful for buying stuff from China. For a central bank to keep its reserves in yuan would be like you keeping your savings in frequent flyer miles. China is giving foreigners and locals alike more freedom to buy and sell yuan, especially in Hong Kong, but it will be a long time before they can buy and sell as much as they please.

As for the euro, are you sure that if you own a 10-year Italian euro bond, Italy won't have abandoned the euro 10 years from now—and repay you in lira?

Thus, the U.S. Treasury bond market is to the world what money market mutual funds are to ordinary investors: a safe, dull place to store cash you need in a hurry. This gives the United States what Valéry Giscard d'Estaing, the French finance minister in 1965, called the *exorbitant privilege* of borrowing astronomical sums in its own currency. If the dollar depreciates, the lender has a problem, not the United States, a point Nixon's Treasury Secretary made in 1971 to the great irritation of the Europeans.

Of course, being inundated with preapproved credit cards also seems like a privilege until the credit card bill arrives. At some point, the United States may wish the

world hadn't let it borrow quite so easily. All that foreign debt has costs, and not just the interest bill that foreigners send us every year. There are political implications, as well.

After Britain and France seized the Suez Canal in 1956, the United States threatened to block an IMF loan to Britain, driving down the pound, if its forces didn't withdraw. Britain complied. Who knows? Maybe China will do to the United States what the United States did to Britain. In other words, if one day China takes a dislike to American foreign policy it may threaten to dump Treasuries, which would perhaps drive up American interest rates. Skeptics note that by hurting its biggest customer this would also hurt China. But then countries routinely put national security ahead of economic expedience: It's why the United States embargoes Cuba. This "balance of financial terror," as Larry Summers called it in a speech in 2004, should keep someone at the Pentagon awake at night.

Into the Weeds

We measure a country's dealings with the rest of the world with the *balance of payments*, which has two sides: the *current account* and the *capital account*. The *current account* includes money we send to foreigners for services

rendered: imports and exports of goods like oil and cars and services like tourism, investment income such as interest on bonds and profits that corporate subsidiaries send back to the head office, and transfers, such as money immigrants send home.

~

Betting on currencies is best left for those with more money than pride.

A country that runs a $10 current account deficit finances it by attracting a net $10 worth of capital; that is, it runs a *capital account* surplus of exactly the same size. Conversely, a country with a current account surplus has to lend to another country or buy its assets.

Each quarter, the Bureau of Economic Analysis releases the balance of payments, which provides a snapshot of global capital movements. (See Table 7.1.) It includes the current account and its components, and the capital account: how much flowed into and out of the country in the form of stocks, bonds, direct investment, and so on. The two are supposed to equal, but seldom do. (Just to confuse you further, these official

government statistics refer to the capital account as the *financial account.*)

Table 7.1 The International Ledger: The Balance of Payments, 2009

Current Account			
Money in		**Money out**	
Exports of goods and services	$1,571 bn	Imports of goods and services	$1,946 bn
Investment receipts (interest, dividends, etc.)	588	Investment payments (interest, dividends, etc.)	467
		Other	125
Total:	2,159	Total:	2,538
Current account deficit: 378*			

Capital Account			
Money in		**Money out**	
Foreign acquisitions of U.S. companies, land, etc.	135	U.S. acquisitions of foreign companies, land, etc.	269
Foreign purchases of Treasuries	584	U.S. purchases of foreign stocks and bonds	208
Other foreign purchases (or sales) of U.S. assets, derivatives	−362	Other U.S. purchases/sales of foreign assets	−336
Total:	357	Total:	140
Capital account surplus: 216*			

*Statistical discrepancy between current and capital accounts: 162.
Source: U.S. Bureau of Economic Analysis.

The Bottom Line

- Global capital markets let investors diversify their portfolios and borrowers choose from different sources of capital. There's a downside, though: Investors' savings may be battered by events in far-off countries, while companies and countries can abruptly have their access to capital cut off.

- The volume of capital flowing across borders far exceeds the volume of trade. Capital can change direction violently, triggering a crisis. The United States borrows cheaply abroad in great part because foreign central banks like to hold dollars: They're safe, easy to convert to other currencies, and backed by a strong, stable country.

Chapter Eight

The Price of Economic Freedom

~

Currencies Reflect a Country's Economic Character, for Better or for Worse

THERE WAS A JOKE making the rounds of trading floors in 2009 that went like this: "What's the difference between Iceland and Ireland? One letter and six months." At the time, these two island nations had a lot in common beyond similar names, and it wasn't flattering. Both

experienced spectacular booms in the early 2000s thanks to banks that grew too fast, and lent too much. In both, the banks then collapsed and economic output shrank roughly 10 percent. In November 2008, Iceland succumbed to the humiliation of an international bailout. Though it took more than six more months (two years, actually), Ireland did, too.

Thereafter, the resemblance ended. By 2012 Iceland's economy was growing briskly and unemployment had eased to 6 percent. Ireland, meanwhile, was barely growing and unemployment was stuck at 14 percent. The most important reason for their divergent paths is that Iceland had its own currency, the krona. During the crisis its value plunged, which eventually boosted exports and tourism. It also led to higher inflation, which reduced the real value of Iceland's debts, making them easier to repay. Ireland, by contrast, had given its own currency up a decade earlier and along with ten other countries, including Germany, adopted the euro. Without its own currency, Ireland couldn't use inflation to reduce its debts or devaluation to boost exports.

The differing experiences of Iceland and Ireland illustrated something people didn't think much about until the euro crisis: why a country's choice of currency matters to its economic prospects.

A currency serves two basic purposes. First, it's a store of value. If you don't want to spend all your

income at once, the part you save needs to be stored somehow. Property, gold, or shares all do fine; cash serves the same purpose, sitting in your wallet or under your mattress until you need it to buy something. Second, a currency is a unit of exchange. Suppose a handyman's son needs braces. In a world without money, he can't pay for them unless the orthodontist needs a new deck. A currency dispenses with barter by enabling everyone to buy and sell in the same unit. A currency can be dollar bills, gold coins, or wampum, so long as it's widely accepted.

Currencies obviously benefit from economies of scale: The more people that use the same currency, the better. Imagine if each of the 50 American states used a different currency. Never mind the hassle of stopping at the foreign exchange booth every time you drove through the Lincoln tunnel. Any transaction that crossed state lines, whether buying a house, taking a job, or signing a contract with a supplier, would carry a whole new element of risk: Will the New York dollar depreciate against the New Jersey dollar? Will the Texas prime rate be higher than the California prime rate? The fact that all 50 states share the dollar makes it infinitely easier to do business while fostering the awareness that all comprise one economy.

But if that's the case, why doesn't the whole world use the same currency? Because no two countries are

alike. Some tolerate faster inflation, less saving, and bigger budget deficits than others. Some are better at employing new technology and management to boost productivity. Some rely on commodities, while others rely on manufactured goods and services, and demand for these things waxes and wanes at different times. Currencies adjust to accommodate these differences. They thus play the same role as any price except on a nationwide scale: to bring the supply and demand for an entire country's goods, services and capital into balance with others.' A country that keeps its own currency thus has more freedom to pursue its own economic path.

Whether a country should have its own currency depends on what's important: the solidarity and efficiency that comes from sharing a currency with another country; or the flexibility of keeping it separate. The architects of the euro thought the first was more important; the crisis that erupted in 2009, a decade after its creation, suggests they underestimated the importance of the second.

What Drives Exchange Rates

Dollars, euros, yen, and pounds lurch about with all the purpose of a toddler in a toy store. Yet there is method to their madness.

In the long run, the most important driver of the exchange rate is inflation. A country that persistently runs higher inflation than its trading partners will see its currency fall as its purchasing power declines. In the 1970s and 1980s Britain's inflation was higher than Germany's, and so the pound declined against Germany's deutsche mark, the currency it used until 2002 when it adopted the euro.*

∼

In the long run, the most important driver of the exchange rate is inflation.

Suppose Britain and Germany both export similar cars, but their prices rise 5 percent a year in Britain because of higher inflation and just 2 percent in Germany. Customers will buy fewer British and more German cars. Demand will decline for the British pound and rise for the deutsche mark. Eventually, the pound will fall enough to make British cars as cheap as German cars again.

*The euro was introduced in 1999 but national notes and coins continued to circulate until 2002.

A related driver of currencies is productivity. Suppose Korean workers and managers find a way to make more ships and televisions with the same number of workers. It would soon be able to sell them more cheaply than its competitors. Korean exporters' sales would rise, earning them more dollars, euros, yen, and francs. As they exchanged those currencies for won to pay their workers and shareholders, the won would rise. Eventually, its increase would cancel out the cost advantage those exporters had achieved through higher productivity.

These two examples show that between two countries, the one with higher productivity growth and lower inflation should have the stronger currency.

If that were the whole story, then big, current account deficits and surpluses should not persist because exchange rates would move to cancel them out. But in fact they can persist, because it's not just the flow of goods and services that determines exchange rates, it's the flow of capital, as well.

Recall from our previous chapter that a country must finance a current account deficit by selling assets, such as stocks, companies, land, or by borrowing (e.g., by issuing bonds). If its assets are in big demand, its currency will remain strong, preventing the current account deficit from correcting itself.

There's lots of great theory behind currency movements, but economists who study them have found that in the short run, the average investor is better off flipping a coin.

While inflation, productivity and savings behavior determine a currency's behavior in the long run, lots of things push it around in the short run.

Interest rates. Countries with higher interest rates attract foreign investors who buy its bonds hoping to earn those higher rates, creating demand for the currency. Lower rates do the opposite. This doesn't work, though, if interest rates are higher only because of inflation. It's the real interest rate (the nominal interest rate minus inflation) that matters.

Economic prospects. When a country's economic outlook improves, its investment opportunities look more attractive and its central bank raises interest rates to stave off inflation. Both those things attract foreign investors, bolstering the currency.

The terms of trade. This is simply the ratio of export prices to import prices. Canada exports a lot

of oil, so when the price of oil goes up, its terms of trade improve. It earns more foreign currency on its exports. Meanwhile, foreign investors rush to buy shares in Canadian oil companies. Both those things create extra demand for Canadian dollars. Thus, rising terms of trade are bullish for a currency.

Greed and fear. Currencies are a real-time indicator of how the world feels about a country, and those feelings can change quite suddenly, from overconfidence to panic. When the world looks like a more dangerous place, because of war or financial meltdown, the political and economic stability of countries such as the United States and Switzerland is particularly appealing and their currencies become safe havens. A country with a rock-solid currency can see it plummet if foreign investors suddenly lose confidence in it.

There's lots of great theory behind currency movements, but economists who study them have found that in the short run, the average investor is better off flipping a coin. People persist in trying, though: The foreign exchange market is the biggest and deepest on the planet and the only one that truly trades around the clock.

Exchange Rate Regimes

For all their advantages, floating exchange rates can be a debilitating source of uncertainty, whether you're a tourist booking your French vacation or a business trying to decide where to open its next branch. And a country with a floating currency may try to drive it down to give its exports a boost at the expense of its trading partners, prompting them to respond in kind.

So countries sometimes try and eliminate the uncertainty of floating exchange rates and the temptation of competitive devaluation by fixing their currencies in some way.

When countries all fixed their currencies to gold, they in effect fixed them to each other, as well. The gold standard collapsed in the 1930s but world leaders resurrected it in modified form under the Bretton Woods agreement, named for the New Hampshire resort where they met in 1944. Participating countries fixed their currencies to the dollar and the United States fixed its dollar to gold; it would convert another country's dollars to gold at $35 per ounce. The International Monetary Fund would police the system, lending money to a country that struggled to finance a current account deficit, and permitting it to devalue if necessary to eliminate the deficit altogether.

The system fell apart when other countries began to acquire large holdings of dollars, often by running trade surpluses with the United States. Eventually, it dawned on everyone that the United States didn't have enough gold to redeem all those dollars. Many countries began converting their dollars to gold, draining American reserves of the metal. In 1971, Richard Nixon shut the gold window: The United States would no longer exchange its gold for dollars. The world entered a period of generally floating exchange rates.

Fixed exchange rates didn't die with Bretton Woods. They are now regularly adopted by individual countries, usually without the consent of the country they peg to. Some do it to control inflation because it eliminates devaluation as the solution to rising costs. Others use it to prevent the currency from rising, thereby maintaining an edge for their exports. More than 60 countries, from China to Belize, peg to the dollar in some way.

The only sure way for a country to lock in an exchange rate is to surrender its monetary passport and adopt another country's currency altogether.

As with any form of price-fixing, a fixed exchange rate won't last if the fundamentals are all wrong, such as excessive inflation or persistent current account deficits. To keep its currency from falling, a central bank must buy it in the open market in exchange for foreign currencies in its reserves. If reserves run low, it has to raise interest rates to persuade investors to buy its currency and prop it up. But it may not have the fortitude to keep rates high if recession threatens. As a last resort, it can impose capital controls, which means people need the government's permission before buying or selling its currency. In 2012 Argentines were banned from converting their savings from pesos to dollars. Tax inspectors deployed dogs trained to sniff out dollars being traded on the street or smuggled out of airports and ferry terminals.

Yet the only sure way for a country to lock in an exchange rate is to surrender its monetary passport and adopt another country's currency altogether.

The Euro

When the nations of Europe emerged from the ashes of World War II, they concluded that one way to avoid a repeat was to become so economically interdependent they would never go to war again. They banded together to form the European Economic Community, which

became the European Union, allowing people and goods to move freely across borders. They also sought to fix their exchange rates to each other. But diverging fundamentals would repeatedly force one or another member to devalue. George Soros made a fortune in 1992 correctly betting the British pound would not stay fixed against the deutsche mark.

The next few years were great for the British economy. The cheaper pound boosted exports, and lower interest rates boosted spending at home. This, of course, did not make Germany happy: Its companies had to labor under a more expensive deutsche mark. To make crises and competitive devaluations a thing of the past, 11 European countries gave up their own currencies and in 1999 adopted the euro to be issued by the European Central Bank. (Eventually six more countries joined; Britain stayed out.) The theory was that without the safety valve of inflation or devaluation, Italians, Spaniards, and Greeks would have to become as thrifty and productive as the Germans. This would take sacrifice, but it was worth it: The more irreversible Europe's economic integration became, the less likely it was to repeat the horror of World War II.

Something surprising happened, though, after the euro was formed. Investors, no longer worried about devaluation, were happy to lend to Greece, Ireland,

Italy, Portugal, and Spain (the so-called GIIPS; for some reason they objected to the original acronym, PIIGS) for only a tiny bit more than they lent to Germany. In some of these countries, households went on a borrowing spree; in others, the government did. Yet their fundamentals did not converge: The GIIPS continued to run higher inflation than Germany, and thus became steadily less competitive. By 2007, they were running a collective current account deficit of $250 billion while Germany was running a surplus of almost exactly the same size.

When Greece in 2009 disclosed the true size of its debts, investors who had lent to these countries or deposited money in their banks began to wonder: How would they get repaid? The buyer of a Treasury bond is confident that she will get back 100 cents on the dollar because Congress can raise taxes to redeem the bond, or, as a last resort, order the Federal Reserve to buy it (I explain how in Chapter 11). California's budget is a perpetual train wreck, but that has never tempted depositors to flee its banks: They sleep easy knowing the federal government insures them. But GIIPS can't order German taxpayers to pay their debts, or the European Union to repay their bank depositors.

Nor can they order the ECB to bail them out by purchasing their bonds. The ECB can only be forced to

do something if all member governments change the Maastricht treaty, which prescribes its goals.

This raised the real threat that one of these countries might default on its bonds, allow its banks to fail, or even leave the euro, repaying creditors in a different, less valuable currency. Fearing one or all of the above, lenders pulled their money out of weak countries' banks and demanded much higher interest rates to compensate for the risk they would get back less than 100 cents on the euro (or something other than a euro).

America's 50 states manage to share a currency without this chaos because they are a fiscal union, not just a monetary union: The federal government taxes and spends on behalf of all the states, narrowing gaps between rich and poor ones. And remember, when the federal government borrows, its bonds, unlike any state's, carry the implicit backing of the central bank. Second, federal deposit insurance means that a state's savers won't be wiped out if its banks fail. Third, the United States is much more economically integrated; people from states with high unemployment regularly move to states with low unemployment. Thus, big gaps in economic performance don't last as long.

Most important, American states are politically united. In the first century of the United States' existence, there was no federal deposit insurance, no

unemployment insurance, social security or Medicaid, and most of the time, no central bank. Individual states regularly endured banking crises and depressions. Some even defaulted on their debts. But none saw that as reason enough to leave the union (slavery was another matter).

For the euro zone to achieve the same cohesion as the United States, its member countries will have to back each other's banks and debts so that their bonds have the same risk-free appeal as U.S. Treasury bonds. But strong countries will only pool risks if in return weak countries surrender sovereignty over their banks and budgets. That will require a political unity the continent has yet to show.

Into the Weeds

If nothing else gets in the way, a product should cost the same in two countries once their prices are converted to the same currency. In practice, they seldom do; but over long periods of time, currencies should move to the theoretical value, called *purchasing power parity*, that would in fact equate the price of a basket of goods in two countries.

There's an important caveat to this. Certain things can't be traded, like visits to the dentist or babysitting. Those things tend to be cheaper in poor countries,

where wages are lower. An American unhappy with the price of her dentist isn't about to order a cheaper one from India. Thus currencies of some countries, especially poor ones, can remain far below purchasing power parity for a long time. It also makes it tricky to compare standards of living. In 2012, per capita income in the United States was $50,000 and in India, just $1,500. But that's converting India's currency, the rupee, to dollars at the going market rate. In fact, $1,500 buys much more in India than in the United States. A better way to compare standards of living is to pretend that currencies were trading at their purchasing power parity. In that case, India's per capita income would be $4,000. In other words, India's standard of living is higher when you look at what its currency can buy in India rather than what it can buy in the United States.

The Bottom Line

- Currencies are both a store of value and a unit of exchange. When regions share a currency, it eases commerce among them. A separate currency, on the other hand, helps countries reconcile differences in inflation, saving, and productivity.

- In the long run, inflation, productivity, and saving are the main drivers of a currency. In the short run, interest rates, economic growth, and the terms of trade dominate.

- To reduce volatility and inflation, one country will often peg its currency to another. But if the fundamentals drive their values apart, the peg will eventually break. Countries may adopt the same currency, as members of the euro zone have done, but if their fundamentals don't converge, the currency union may not last.

All the President's Men

~

They Don't Control the Economy but They Sure Do Try

PRESIDENTS LIVE OR DIE by the economy. If you tracked public disapproval of the president against the unemployment rate, you'd see they move closely together. Unfortunately, being held responsible for the economy isn't the same as being able to do something about it. Economic growth is the product of countless unorchestrated actions by business, consumers, innovators, investors, and government at home and abroad. A president may get a change in taxes or spending through

Congress, but the effect on growth is often fleeting and hard to detect. The government agency with the most immediate, tangible influence on the economy, the Federal Reserve, is also the one the president is least able to push around.

Even when a president's policies do change the economy, they may not show results for years, and then, not the intended ones.

For instance, the inflation that Gerald Ford and Jimmy Carter struggled with began with mistakes by their predecessors, Lyndon Johnson and Richard Nixon. The deregulation often attributed to Ronald Reagan actually began under Carter. The Internet revolution that buoyed the economy in Bill Clinton's last years in office could be traced to the Defense Department's development of a dispersed communications network in the 1950s and 1960s that could survive battlefield conditions. And who's to blame for the financial crisis that made the last years of George W. Bush's presidency and Barack Obama's so miserable? You'd have to finger a litany of unconnected regulatory and political decisions stretching back two and a half decades.

Still, presidential decisions do matter for individuals, companies, and industries, and if done right, they can help the economy grow faster and spread the fruits of that growth to more people.

~

**Presidents populate their administrations
with economic experts whose influence
depends on their personal rapport
with the president and the president's
willingness to listen.**

The Company Presidents Keep

A president implements economic policy both through his own decisions, aided by a network of advisors and government departments, and through the people he appoints to run regulatory agencies.

Presidents populate their administrations with economic experts whose influence depends on their personal rapport with the president and the president's willingness to listen. Inevitably, the economic advisors compete to be heard with political advisors, Congress, and the president's own predispositions, and they often don't win. The economic experts themselves may disagree. When the little-known economist, George Warren, persuaded Franklin D. Roosevelt to take the United States off the gold standard, another adviser called it "the end of western civilization." History, however, shows that Warren was right.

—————————————— ～ ——————————————

**With a staff of 25, the National Economic
Council is one of Washington's smallest
economic agencies yet potentially
its most powerful.**

——

Of the numerous agencies that give the president
economic advice, four are key.

1. **National Economic Council (NEC).** With a
 staff of 25, the National Economic Council is
 one of Washington's smallest, yet most powerful
 economic agencies. Clinton created the NEC in
 1993 and named Robert Rubin as its first direc-
 tor. From a warren of offices in the West Wing of
 the White House, the NEC filters the economic
 advice that pours in from the rest of
 the administration and presents its findings and
 recommendations to the president.

2. **The Office of Management and Budget
 (OMB).** The Office of Management and Budget
 develops the president's fiscal and budget policy.
 The OMB director's job boils down to finding a
 way to fit a gigantic expanse of budget requests
 into the straitjacket of projected tax revenue. This

means both weighing in on high-profile initiatives and screening government agencies' many mundane budget requests.

One of the OMB director's main jobs is to say no to the constant demands for more spending or lower taxes from Congress and other agencies. But, the fact remains: Budget directors are routinely overruled by political priorities.

The OMB's Office of Information and Regulatory Affairs screens the regulations issued by other federal agencies, from the Environmental Protection Agency to the Food and Drug Administration. If it thinks a regulation is poorly formulated or justified, it can send it back. The OMB also oversees the nuts and bolts of how the government and the civil service are run.

3. **Council of Economic Advisers (CEA).** The Council of Economic Advisers is the president's in-house think tank. It is a creature of the Employment Act of 1946 and that era's utopian belief that good economics can produce better government. The CEA is peopled mostly by itinerant economists plucked from academia or think tanks for two- to four-year stints. The council's three members, one of whom is chairman, have included some of the country's best-known

economists, including James Tobin, Burton Malkiel, Alan Greenspan, Joseph Stiglitz, and Ben Bernanke. It is a nonpartisan rite of passage for many of the country's most promising economists. Paul Krugman and Larry Summers, though both Democrats, worked for Martin Feldstein, the Republican chairman of Reagan's CEA.

4. **The Treasury**. Created in Congress' first session in 1789, the Treasury is the oldest and arguably most prestigious federal department and the only one with its own tunnel to the White House. Secretaries of the Treasury have always been among the most prominent cabinet members, starting with the first, Alexander Hamilton. The Treasury's formal responsibilities are quite prosaic: It collects taxes and manages the national debt.

Informally, the Treasury Secretary's main job is chief economic spokesman of the administration and indeed the country.

In the competition for the president's ear, the Treasury Secretary has formidable advantages: a gigantic staff of experts and desk officers and regular, high-profile meetings with finance ministers and central bankers from around the world. The Treasury Secretary

—— ∽ ——

**Most federal regulators are independent but
their actions still reflect the inclinations of
the political appointees who run them.**

is official spokesman on the dollar, and traders cling to
his words like burrs to his clothes.

The Long Arms of the Law

The president's economic advisors are the public face of
his economic policy. Yet many of the most momentous
economic decisions emerge from regulatory agencies.
There are some 50 such agencies from the National
Labor Relations Board to the Office of Pipeline Safety.
Most are independent in that they enforce rules defined
in law rather than follow the dictates of the president
or Congress, but how they interpret the law reflects the
inclinations of the people who run the agencies and
the politicians who appoint them.

Free markets are unequaled at channeling capital
and labor to their most productive purposes. The fed-
eral government has not always believed that. From
the 1930s to the 1970s its heavy hand decided who
could compete in industries ranging from telecommu-
nications to airlines and what prices they could charge.
It made for stable, predictable business, but squelched

competition and innovation and kept prices artificially high.

Starting in the 1970s, deregulation and antitrust lawsuits swept away most overt economic controls. Airlines and truckers are free to compete on any route for any price—and frequently go bankrupt in the process. AT&T's telephone monopoly is long gone. Banks can pay depositors any interest rate they like.

In the social sphere, however, the list of new rules grows steadily, to protect the environment, safety, privacy and national security; and prevent discrimination, monopolistic behavior, fraud, and terrorist attacks.

There's a solid economic rationale for such rules. Private transactions often carry a social cost. For example, a utility that pollutes the air imposes a cost on everyone nearby who breathes. Good regulations force private buyers and sellers to internalize those social costs. Emissions controls raise the price of electricity, leaving customers worse off, but society better off. Of course, rules have less quantifiable costs and benefits: Fuel efficiency standards restrict consumers' choices while also reducing dependence on oil imported from odious regimes. New rules may consume so much of business' attention that they put off hiring and investing. To determine the right trade-off, the federal government often subjects rules to cost-benefit analysis. Still,

the process is incomplete and subjective, guaranteeing that regulation will always be one of the most contentious fields of economic policy.

For the economy, the most important regulators are those overseeing the financial system because they can determine how freely and safely credit flows.

In 2010 the Dodd-Frank act completely overhauled financial regulation with the aim of preventing the abuses and oversights that led to the crisis of 2007 to 2009. Whether it succeeds, no one is sure, in part because the law will take time to implement and even then can't anticipate all future problems.

At the top of the new regulatory hierarchy sits the Financial Stability Oversight Council, chaired by the Treasury Secretary. Its 10 members include the heads of most federal regulators. The FSOC looks for risks to the financial system, tries to get individual regulators to cooperate and share information, and designates "systemically important financial institutions" (SIFIs) that are so large, their failure could threaten the financial system.

U.S. bank regulation is ridiculously complicated. Some banks are state chartered and some are federally chartered. Most are owned by holding companies that might have lots of other subsidiaries that aren't banks.

This has resulted in a sprawling collection of regulators, including:

- **The Federal Reserve.** As the big dog of economic regulators, it regulates bank-holding companies like Citigroup Inc. and JPMorgan Chase & Co. and state-chartered banks that are members of the Federal Reserve system. It also regulates SIFIs.

- **The Office of the Comptroller of the Currency (OCC).** The OCC regulates nationally chartered banks, which includes most of the biggest banks, like Citibank. In 2011, the OCC absorbed the Office of Thrift Supervision (OTS). The OTS formerly supervised thrift banks (also known as savings and loans), though not very well.

- **The Federal Deposit Insurance Corporation (FDIC).** The FDIC regulates state-chartered banks that aren't part of the Federal Reserve system and runs the deposit insurance fund.

- **State Banking Departments.** These share the regulation of state-chartered banks with the Fed and the FDIC.

Alongside these bank regulators, there are several others:

- **The Securities and Exchange Commission (SEC).** The SEC regulates securities brokers and dealers, mutual funds, and stock exchanges

like the New York Stock Exchange and Nasdaq Stock Market. It also polices investment advisors, credit rating agencies, and any company whose shares trade on a stock market to ensure its financial statements comply with the law.

- **The Commodity Futures Trading Commission (CFTC).** The CFTC regulates derivatives, such as futures contracts on corn, Eurodollars, and oil; the exchanges on which they trade, like the Chicago Mercantile Exchange and the Intercontinental Exchange; and the firms that trade them. It also regulates swaps, which are similar to futures but don't trade on exchanges.

- **The Consumer Financial Protection Bureau (CFPB).** In 2011 the CFPB took over responsibility for consumer protection from the bank regulators. It writes and enforces rules governing consumer financial products such as mortgages and credit cards.

- **Federal Housing Finance Agency.** This agency regulates Fannie Mae and Freddie Mac, two formerly privately owned companies that own and guarantee mortgages. They were placed in "conservatorship," a form of receivership, by the Treasury Department in 2008. It also regulates the 12 Federal Home Loan Banks, which lend to, and are owned by, banks.

The federal government enforces the rules of the free market at home through competition laws. Two agencies lead the effort: the Federal Trade Commission (FTC) and the Department of Justice through its Antitrust Division. They enforce the Sherman Antitrust Act of 1890, which prohibits anticompetitive behavior and monopolies; the Clayton Act of 1914, which prohibits anticompetitive mergers; and the Hart-Scott-Rodino Act of 1976, which requires mergers be scrutinized for competitive impact. Although the two share many duties such as reviewing mergers and investigating anticompetitive conduct, there are some differences. Only the Justice Department can bring criminal charges, and the FTC has broader power to investigate questionable business practices and consumer complaints.

The FTC and the Justice Department investigate things like cartelization, price-fixing, bid-rigging, and illegal monopoly. In theory, the antitrust laws are nonpartisan but in practice, different administrations pursue these things differently. For example, Democrats are fonder of breaking up corporate monopolies or oligopolies in hopes of bringing down costs and fostering competition, while Republicans are more likely to trust market forces to loosen any would-be monopolist's grip. Thus, the Clinton Administration pursued Microsoft for years for its alleged anticompetitive behavior, but the Bush Administration settled the case with just a slap on the wrist.

The globalization of business means antitrust rulings increasingly reach across borders. In the past decade, the European Union's competition commissioner has become a force to be reckoned with by U.S. companies; it killed General Electric's merger with Honeywell and kept up its investigation of Microsoft long after the United States dropped its own.

The Bottom Line

- Presidents don't control the economy but they sure try. A president's economic agenda is dictated by ideology, but how it is implemented depends on the circle of economic advisers in the National Economic Council, the Treasury Department, the Office of Management and Budget, and the Council of Economic Advisers.

- Presidents also exercise a lot of influence through their appointments to dozens of federal regulatory agencies. The bank regulators, for example, influence who gets credit and under what terms while the Justice Department and the Federal Trade Commission set the ground rules for business conduct and competition.

- Regulation that dictates which firms can compete and the prices they charge has largely retreated, while regulation over safety, the environment, and other social goals has grown.

Chapter Ten

The Buck Starts Here

~

*The Federal Reserve's Amazing
Power to Print and Destroy Money*

BACK IN 1986, *NEWSWEEK* called the Federal Reserve chairman the second most powerful man in America. In the financial crisis of 2007 to 2009, you could delete the word *second* as the Fed, under its chairman Ben Bernanke, cut interest rates, propped up banks, lent to cash-strapped companies, and bought hundreds of billions of dollars of mortgages to keep the economy from collapsing.

The Fed occupies a unique position in the United States. It is a partly public, partly private institution whose political independence rivals the Supreme Court's. It is populated by technocratic central bankers who, regardless of party affiliation, see themselves as united in their mission of low inflation and steady growth. They speak their own nerdy dialect, "Fedspeak," saying things like *monetary accommodation* instead of *low interest rates*. They revel in goofy inside jokes. A sign in the Fed's barbershop reads, "Your growth rate affects my money supply."

Spandex Money

The United States struggled for years over whether to have a central bank. Alexander Hamilton, the first secretary of the Treasury, convinced Congress to create the First Bank of the United States in 1791 to handle the infant republic's monetary affairs, over the objections of then-Secretary of State Thomas Jefferson, who feared the concentration of so much economic power in one place. Hostility to the bank persisted and in 1811 Congress let its charter lapse. The Second Bank of the United States began life in 1816, but Andrew Jackson, a populist opposed to the power of money interests, vetoed the renewal of its charter, which expired in 1836.

~

The event that finally led to the Fed's creation was the Panic of 1907.

Without a central bank, private and state-owned banks could issue their own currencies, convertible in theory on demand to gold. In practice, one bank's dollar might be worth more than another's if investors had more faith in its stability. Banks seldom kept enough gold to redeem all the currency they issued; they would borrow from other, usually bigger, banks to handle contingencies. But if many banks faced the same demand at once, there wouldn't be enough gold to go around. As a result, many banks failed. Customers, fearing others would follow, would then rush to convert their notes to gold, triggering more failures. Such panics were commonplace.

The event that finally led to the Fed's creation was the Panic of 1907, which began with a run on several banks that had lost money when customers speculated in the stock market. John Pierpont Morgan, the head of the bank that bore his name, convened New York's leading bankers in his personal library and persuaded them to meet all the demands for cash then besieging

the city's troubled banks. To prevent a repeat, Congress, at the prodding of banks, passed the Federal Reserve Act in 1913.

The act said that the Fed's job was to furnish an "elastic currency." This does not mean it prints $20 bills on spandex; rather, it means expanding and shrinking the money supply as needed. This gives the Fed two powerful roles:

1. **Lender of last resort.** A bank that has run out of money to repay its creditors can borrow from the Fed. (In Chapter 12, I show how the Fed does this.)
2. **Carrying out monetary policy.** By manipulating the supply of dollars to banks, the Fed can raise or lower interest rates with the goal of holding down inflation and preventing recessions, a set of responsibilities called *monetary policy*. (In Chapter 11, I discuss this in detail.)

The Fed, over the long run, can't make the economy grow more quickly or produce more jobs; that depends on population and productivity. But in the short run, monetary policy gives it tremendous influence over the business cycle. Higher interest rates dampen spending by households and businesses and

thus economic growth, eventually, restraining prices and wages. Conversely, lower interest rates stimulate spending and, with time, put upward pressure on prices and wages.

Yet, despite these powers and its leaders' earnest idealism, the Fed's efforts to steer the economy by fulfilling those two roles are often upended by bubbles, busts, inflation, deflation, oil embargoes, technology revolutions, and more, as an overview of its history reveals.

In its early years, the Fed sought to merely meet farmers' and industry's demand for credit without influencing the overall temper of economic activity. When farmers needed money to bring the harvest in, the Fed expanded the money supply so that banks could meet their needs. Then, when the farmers repaid their loans, the money supply contracted. By the 1920s, though, the Fed had gotten more ambitious, seeking to influence nationwide economic activity and inflation with interest rates.

In its history, the Fed has made two monumental mistakes. The first began in the late 1920s. Worried that speculation in the stock market was creating a dangerous bubble, it jacked up interest rates. This sharply slowed the economy down. In October of 1929, the overheated stock market finally crashed. The Fed initially cut interest rates but then stood by as banks in the

United States and around the world collapsed, unleashing a devastating contraction of credit. Precisely why remains a matter of debate. Its willingness to hold down interest rates and expand credit was inhibited by a fear that foreigners would respond by dumping their dollars and demanding gold in return, draining the Fed's essential supply of the metal, though it had plenty. Regardless of the cause, the Great Depression bottomed out in 1933 when Franklin D. Roosevelt used a bank holiday to close dying banks and recapitalize the remainder, and devalued the dollar against gold.

From the late 1940s to the late 1960s, the Fed kept growth strong, recessions short, and inflation generally low. By the late 1960s, though, its effort to keep the economy at full employment led to its second monumental mistake. It repeatedly failed to raise interest rates enough to stop inflation from ratcheting higher. Inflation and recession ensued in the 1970s. In reaction to those failures, in 1978, Congress imposed its current mandate on the Fed: full employment, stable prices, and moderate long-term interest rates.

❧

Before the crisis, Congress paid the Fed the
ultimate compliment by ignoring it.

The modern era of the Fed began in 1979 with the appointment of Paul Volcker as chairman. He promptly raised interest rates and induced two severe recessions, breaking the back of inflation. The years spanning from 1982 to 2007 became known as the "Great Moderation," a period marked by generally low inflation, declining unemployment rates, and just two mild recessions. Central bankers thought they'd uncovered the holy grail of economic success—deliver low inflation and the economy will grow. Everything else would take care of itself. By 2006, when Bernanke succeeded Alan Greenspan as chairman, things were going so swimmingly that Congress paid the Fed the ultimate compliment: It ignored it. When someone asked a senator what he thought of Bernanke's nomination, he replied, "for what?" Seriously.

The Fed is a compromise between federally appointed officials in Washington and autonomous reserve banks controlled by private bankers.

Less than two years after Bernanke took office, the Great Moderation and the Fed's aura of technocratic

competence ended with the financial crisis and recession of 2007 to 2009. The Fed shares the blame for the crisis, because of its prior lax regulation of banks and mortgages and, according to some, holding interest rates as low as it did, contributing to speculation and the housing boom.

Who's in Charge?

It is a bedrock principle of modern economics that those who spend the public's money should not be allowed to print it. Thus, central banks should be as independent as possible. On the other hand, central banks have enormous influence over the public's welfare. So how to balance independence with public accountability?

The Fed's governance reflects a compromise at its birth in 1913 between populists who wanted power to rest with federally appointed officials in Washington, and conservatives who wanted it to rest with autonomous reserve banks controlled by private bankers. The system split power between a politically appointed board in Washington and 12 regional reserve banks.

In 1935, the structure was overhauled to shift power from the 12 reserve banks to the governors. That structure persists today. The seven-member board of governors sets all Fed policy except monetary policy. For

example, it interprets and applies laws governing banks. The president nominates and the senate confirms governors, and from among those governors, the chairman and two vice-chairmen: One fills in when the chairman is away and the other oversees bank supervision. Governors are appointed to staggered 14-year terms to insulate them from political pressure (although few serve the full 14 years). The chairman and vice-chairmen serve four-year terms. In theory, a chairman whose term expires can remain a governor.

The 12 regional reserve banks are stationed across the United States and are charged with supervising local banks, distributing cash, and processing checks. The boundaries of the districts they oversee defy geographic logic; two banks are based in Missouri partly because it was the home state of the speaker of the House in 1913. Each bank has nine directors: three represent banks, three business, and three the rest of the public. The latter six appoint the reserve bank presidents. The most important reserve bank is New York, whose 400-strong markets group carries out the daily financial transactions that alter interest rates, lend to banks, and occasionally push the dollar up or down.

This hybrid public-private structure works well at insulating the Fed from most political pressure, but not completely. Lyndon Johnson and Richard Nixon both

pressured Fed chairmen to keep interest rates low, with some success. Ronald Reagan appointed governors who sought to corral the power of Paul Volcker. George H. W. Bush sought to influence Greenspan by briefly withholding reappointment (it didn't work). Congress plays the game, too, by refusing to confirm the president's governor nominees or by threatening to clip the Fed's wings. And it can always amend the Federal Reserve Act.

Monetary policy is the exclusive purview of the 12-member Federal Open Market Committee (FOMC). All seven members of the board of governors and the New York Fed president sit on the FOMC. The four remaining seats rotate annually among the 11 other reserve bank presidents. Though only five presidents vote, all 12 participate in FOMC meetings so the FOMC is commonly thought of as having 19 members: 12 voting and 7 nonvoting.

Fed chairmen, though political appointees, are usually technocrats rather than partisans and lead through the persuasiveness of their argument rather than the force of their personality. Bernanke was an accomplished monetary policy scholar at Princeton University when George W. Bush appointed him a Fed governor in 2002. He briefly served as chairman of Bush's Council of Economic Advisers in 2005. In February of 2006, he succeeded Greenspan as Fed chairman.

~

Bernanke didn't much care for the
New Deal but he admired Roosevelt's
willingness to try anything to get the
economy going. Bernanke has shown a
similar willingness to experiment.

In *Essays on the Great Depression*, Bernanke wrote, "I
am a Great Depression buff, the way some people are
Civil War buffs." He blames the Depression on the
Fed's misguided adherence to orthodoxy, which caused
it to stand by as the economy collapsed. Bernanke didn't
much care for the New Deal but he admired Roosevelt's
willingness to try anything to get the economy going.
Bernanke showed a similar willingness to experiment in
tackling the crisis and recession of 2007 to 2009 and
their aftermath.

Bernanke, as he later described it, "was not going to
be the Federal Reserve chairman who presided over
the second Great Depression." He pushed the limits of the
Fed's powers to lend to all and sundry, slash interest
rates, and buy up bonds. Bernanke's aggressive actions
stirred up suspicions of central bank power and were
harshly criticized by some politicians. That's why the
Fed is independent: to do what it must, no matter how
unpopular.

The Bottom Line

- The Fed stands alone in its economic sway and its independence. It can print and destroy money at will to protect the financial system from panics and to manage the business cycle.

- The Fed is a compromise between political accountability and private independence. Its politically appointed governors and privately appointed reserve bank presidents make up the Federal Open Market Committee, which sets monetary policy at meetings eight times a year.

Chapter Eleven

White Smoke over the Washington Mall

The Making of Monetary Policy and the Fine Art of Fed Watching

MORE THAN ALMOST ANY other event on the economic calendar, meetings of the Federal Open Market Committee (FOMC) have the potential to rattle the markets. No wonder, then, that they are so closely watched.

One of those meetings was scheduled to wrap up December 16, 2008. The financial crisis was still raging

and the economy deep in recession. The news that morning was particularly bad: Housing construction had fallen to an all-time low and consumer prices were flirting with deflation. The news investors most wanted, though, was what would the Federal Reserve do about this sorry picture? That afternoon, they got their answer: pretty much everything. The Fed announced it would "employ all available tools" to revive the economy: It cut its main interest rate from 1 percent to nearly zero; committed to keeping it there for "some time"; promised to buy truckloads of mortgage-backed bonds; and said Treasury bonds could be next. The announcement hit markets like a bolt of lightning. The stock market rocketed higher, while bond yields and the dollar plummeted.

That day illustrated several important things about monetary policy. It affects the economic outlook like nothing else can. It takes many shapes, from changing interest rates and verbal nods to purchases of all sorts of bonds. And for all its potency, it may not be enough.

Inside the FOMC Meeting

For all their market-moving potential, meetings of the FOMC are staid affairs generally bereft of drama. Eight times a year, the 19 members of the FOMC gather in Washington for a two-day meeting. The Fed chairman

sits at the center of the table, the other 18 members (assuming there are no vacancies) sit on either side, their nameplates riveted on the back of their seat. They review conditions in financial markets, the staff's economic forecast, and then debate options about what monetary policy actions to take. Finally, the chairman makes a recommendation and calls a vote. After the meeting wraps up, members help themselves to a buffet lunch. At either 12:30 or 2:15 P.M., the committee issues its statement.

FOMC members can be classified as hawks or doves. Hawks generally prefer tighter policy than their peers, are more vocal, and are more likely to cast a dissenting vote. Why are hawks so much more outspoken than doves? It's a matter of professional pride. A central banker would rather be known for his toughness on inflation than his concern for unemployment. "Only hawks get to go to central banker heaven," Robert McTeer, a Dallas Fed president, once said. Doves are more likely to worry about unemployment, and to think that inflation worries are overdone. A central banker with dovish tendencies is like a wine critic who drinks Merlot out of a box. Nothing wrong with it, but best kept behind closed doors.

An FOMC member who is one of the 12 reserve bank presidents (other than New York's) is more likely

to dissent than one of the governors. That's because governors share offices, staff, and a sense of solidarity with the chairman. Still, unlike on the Supreme Court, close FOMC votes are unheard of. Inflation and unemployment can animate economics geeks for hours but are much less divisive than the things the Supreme Court grapples with like abortion, freedom of speech, and the rights of suspected terrorists. The Fed traditionally prefers consensus so the chairman, unlike the Chief Justice of the Supreme Court, carries the day by default. More than two dissents is rare. Laurence Meyer, a former governor, once joked that there are two red chairs at the table. Only members in red chairs get to dissent.

Punch Bowls and Ham Sandwiches

William McChesney Martin, a former Fed chairman, famously described the Fed's role as taking away the punch bowl just when the party gets going. FOMC deliberations are consumed by figuring out just how much punch to supply. If everyone is having a good time spending money, the Fed cools things down by taking the punch bowl away, that is, by raising interest rates. The opposite is also true: If spending is moribund, it is the Fed's job to supply as much punch as necessary to get the people to come to party in the first place.

Calibrating the punch supply involves several delicate judgments:

- How far is the economy operating from its productive capacity, which is its potential output? In other words, how big is the output gap? A related question is how far is unemployment from its natural rate?
- How far is inflation from the Fed's target?
- What's the outlook for these two things given the forecast for growth, unemployment, and the public's expectations of inflation?

Price stability is a term of art. Right now, the Fed defines it as 2 percent inflation.

As I described in Chapter 5, both potential growth and the natural rate of unemployment are rather hard to nail down. And any Fed chairman who wanted to keep his job would think twice before asserting publicly that *any* level of unemployment was natural. Fortunately, the Fed makes it possible for a careful reader to discern its estimates of both potential growth and the natural rate

of unemployment. Four times a year, the Fed publishes the collective forecasts of FOMC members for major economic indicators. Their long-run forecast of growth roughly corresponds to their estimate of potential growth (from 2.3 to 2.5 percent) while their long-run forecast of unemployment corresponds to their estimate of the natural rate of unemployment (from 5.2 to 6 percent).

"Price stability" is one of the Fed's goals, but historically that was a term of art; price stability was whatever inflation rate the Fed wished. Then in 2012 it announced that henceforth it considered price stability to be inflation of 2 percent. How does this target work? In ordinary times, if inflation is, or expected to be, over 2 percent, the Fed might raise interest rates so that the economy operates below potential long enough for it to fall back. If inflation instead is below 2 percent, it might lower interest rates until the economy is operating above potential long enough to bring it back. But the Fed treats this target flexibly and doesn't automatically respond when inflation deviates from 2 percent; for one thing, the Fed must keep an eye on its other goal of full employment. For another, inflation bounces around for lots of reasons and deviations from 2 percent may not last.

One thing the Fed doesn't dwell on is the money supply; it's not much use for predicting inflation or

economic growth. The Fed did explicitly target the money supply from 1979 to 1982. Currently, though, entire meetings regularly transpire with no mention of the money supply—despite that sign in the barber shop.

Generally, the further the economy is operating below its capacity, the lower the FOMC will keep interest rates in an effort to get it back up. The higher inflation is relative to its target, the higher it will keep interest rates. The Fed's job sounds simple, right? Estimate the output gap, check on inflation, set interest rates, go golfing. May as well replace the Fed with a ham sandwich.

It's harder than it sounds. Monetary policy works with long and variable lags because loan, wage, and price contracts take a while to change. The quarterback throws to where the receiver will be when the ball arrives, not where he is when the ball is thrown. Similarly, the Fed aims its actions at where the economy and inflation are headed over the next one to three years. All these decisions are prone to error. Potential is unknowable, the future is a guess, and the past isn't much easier given how often data is revised. People are unpredictable: If rates rise, they may buy fewer homes, or they may buy more if they think even higher rates are on the way.

Things have also gotten infinitely harder since the recession of 2007 to 2009, which, as we will see, forced

the Fed to use unconventional tools to deal with an unprecedented combination of high unemployment and low inflation.

∾

**Nowadays it is hard to shut the Fed up:
It spews forth a virtually continuous gusher
of information and commentary.**

Fedspeak

What the Fed says is almost as important as what it does. It wasn't always that way. Before the 1990s, the Fed followed the credo of Montagu Norman, a Bank of England governor: "Never explain, never apologize." It rarely disclosed changes in interest rates; therefore, investors deciphered such changes from the Fed's market operations. It believed that talking caused unnecessary volatility, and if it discussed what it might do, it would bind its hands if a different course of action proved necessary.

Starting in the early 1990s, this fondness for opacity changed. The Fed now believes that talking actually harnesses the markets to its own ends. Fret aloud about

inflation and bond yields will rise, doing some of the Fed's work for it. In fact, it's hard to shut the Fed up: It spews forth a virtually continuous gusher of information and commentary. The most important is the statement that the FOMC releases at the end of each meeting. It usually provides the interest rate decision, a description of the economy and its outlook, a hint of where interest rates will go next, and how the FOMC members voted.

Three weeks after each meeting, the Fed releases detailed minutes disclosing more of the reasoning and debate behind the decision, without naming who said what. A full transcript follows five years later. Between meetings, members give speeches. Several times a year, the chairman testifies to Congress; in February and July this testimony is accompanied by a lengthy *Monetary Policy Report*. Four times a year, the FOMC releases its members' projections of growth, unemployment, inflation, and where they expect interest rates to go. Following those meetings, the chairman holds a press conference. Officials also give interviews, often off the record, to reporters who then try to infer the Fed's next move.

Not all Fed pronouncements are created equal. The chairman's matters the most because he speaks for

the entire FOMC. Those of habitual hawks and doves matter least because their views seldom change with the circumstances. Savvy Fed watchers pay close attention to officials known to influence the chairman's thinking (the vice-chair, for example) or who are open to persuasion when the chairman is mustering support. With all this Fedspeak, the Fed's actions are less likely to shock people.

Once the FOMC has decided what to do, it must execute the policy. Before 2008, the Fed operated principally with the conventional tool of short-term interest rates. After cutting interest rates close to zero at that meeting in December 2008, it turned to unconventional tools. We'll examine both separately.

Into the Weeds, Conventionally

Until 2008, the FOMC's decision was simple: What will be its target for the Federal Funds rate, the rate that banks charge on one-day loans to each other? The Fed Funds rate is a benchmark for all other short-term rates: the bank prime rate, commercial paper, Treasury bills, and floating-rate mortgages. It also ripples through to long-term bond yields and mortgage rates, although the effect is more muted, because bond investors lend for years, not just a few days or weeks. It can also affect stock prices and the dollar. With this one modest

interest rate lever, the Fed sways an array of financial conditions, and thus the entire economy.

Once the FOMC selects a target for the Fed Funds rate, it has to manage market conditions to make the rate at which banks exchange money actually meet that target. It does this through *open market operations*. To understand how these work, start with the fact that banks are required to keep a portion of customers' deposits readily available as cash in their vaults or ATMs, or as deposits at the Fed, which are called *reserves*. Banks use reserves to settle payments with each other and with the Treasury, for example as customers cash Social Security checks or pay their taxes. The daily flow of such payments may leave one bank with more reserves than it needs, and another with less. The first can lend its excess to the second in the Fed Funds market.

To lower the Fed Funds rate, the Fed's open market desk in New York buys Treasury securities, or securities backed by Fannie Mae or Freddie Mac, from a bank or the bank's customer. To pay for them, it creates money out of thin air, which it deposits in the bank's reserve account with the Fed. This is, de facto, printing money, because the bank is free to swap those reserves for notes and coins. These operations expand the Fed's balance sheet. With more reserves than it needs, the bank lends some out, pushing down the Fed Funds rate.

To raise the Fed Funds rate, the Fed does the opposite: It sells securities from its own portfolio. The bank that buys them pays the Fed out of its reserve account. That money disappears and the Fed's balance sheet shrinks. That bank, to replenish its reserves, borrows from other banks, pushing up the Federal Funds rate.

Into the Weeds, Unconventionally

When the Fed dropped the Federal Funds target to between zero and 0.25 percent in December 2008, it was widely said to be out of bullets.

A soldier out of bullets still has bayonets, knives, and grenades. So does the Fed; let's look at them in turn.

- **Open mouth operations**. The Federal Funds rate is charged on one-day loans; someone about to lend for several years wants to know what that rate will be in the future. The Fed can affect those expectations with verbal guidance. For example, it said in August 2011 that the funds rate would likely stay near zero at least two more years. Ten-year Treasury bond yields and 30-year mortgage rates both fell about a fifth of a percentage point.
- **Quantitative easing**. Basic finance tells us that when the price of a bond goes up, its yield—the long-term

interest rate—goes down* (and vice versa). The Fed can reduce long-term interest rates by purchasing bonds, elevating their prices. How does it pay for those bonds? As with conventional open-market operations it creates money out of thin air that it deposits in banks' reserve accounts. But unlike with conventional policy, it is targeting a particular quantity of bonds and reserves, so this is called *quantitative easing*. Between the end of 2007 and mid-2012, the Fed more than tripled its holdings of securities to $2.6 trillion while banks' reserves went from, in effect, nothing to $1.5 trillion. In theory, the Fed could buy every bond in existence this way.

- **Operation Twist**. The Fed can buy bonds and instead of paying for them by creating money, it can sell shorter-term bonds and Treasury bills already in its portfolio. The Fed and Treasury tried something similar in the 1960s in an attempt to "twist" the structure of interest rates. It was called *Operation Twist* after the dance craze inspired by the eminent economist Chubby Checker.
- **Credit easing**. The Fed can affect different interest rates by buying different types of bonds.

*A $100 bond that pays a $5 coupon every year has a yield of 5 percent. Suppose the price rises to $125; the yield represented by that $5 coupon falls to 4 percent.

Buying mortgage backed securities, for example, pushes down mortgage rates more than just buying Treasuries. Such targeted easing is especially helpful if shell-shocked investors shun a particular type of borrower, such as home buyers or small businesses.

- **Negative interest rates**. Instead of paying banks interest on their reserves, the Fed could charge banks a fee, as central banks in Denmark and Sweden have done. This would be the same as a negative interest rate and might encourage banks to lend the money out. Banks could pass the fee on to their own depositors, who would thus be encouraged to spend. But if interest rates became negative enough, everyone would simply hold cash and hire security guards.

- **Foreign exchange intervention**. When the Fed buys a foreign currency, its value rises while the dollar falls. This boosts exports and dampens imports. The Fed does this rarely, and when it does, it pays for the currency with dollars that it borrows. It would be much more powerful if the Fed simply printed the dollars. Both Japan and Switzerland have tried such "unsterilized intervention." But it's controversial: The benefits come at the rest of the world's expense. Indeed, the United States is always lecturing other countries not to do precisely this.

Unconventional policy works much as the conventional sort does: Lower long-term interest rates encourage people to borrow and spend, just as lower short term rates do. But it may also prompt investors to alter their portfolios. Just as taking soda machines out of high schools should encourage students to drink milk, reducing the supply of government bonds encourages investors to put their money somewhere else, for example into corporate bonds and stocks. Hopefully that boosts investment and makes people feel wealthier.

But there are risks with unconventional policies:

- **Inflation**. When people hear the Fed is printing money, they assume inflation will follow. As we saw in Chapter 5, that's wrong: For the new money to cause inflation, it must be lent and spent. QE should eventually raise spending, but the Fed would have plenty of time to reverse course before inflation truly threatened. Of course, that may not stop people from worrying about inflation; they may rush to buy oil or gold as a hedge. Higher oil prices would hurt.

- **Exit strategy**. QE complicates matters when the Fed eventually raises interest rates again. To raise the Federal Funds rate, the Fed ordinarily reduces the supply of reserves. That's easy when banks don't have many reserves, hard when they

have more than $1 trillion. Luckily, the Fed has a fallback: It can pay interest on excess reserves (IOER). If it wants a Federal Funds rate of 3 percent, it can raise IOER to 3 percent. If banks earn 3 percent from the Fed, they won't lend to each other in the Fed Funds market for less.

- **Politics.** When the Fed buys government bonds, it is lending to the government. This is called *monetizing the debt*. Even though politicians didn't force the Fed to buy the bonds, some experts look at the soaring national debt and worry that eventually they will. For that to happen, FOMC members would have to surrender their independence or have it taken away by Congress. Both are pretty unlikely; in fact many in Congress oppose QE precisely because they think it's bailing out the government.

- **Distorting markets.** Unconventional policy mucks up the machinery of finance. Money market funds, for example, can't cover their expenses with interest rates of zero. If they closed up shop, where would the companies that sell short-term IOUs to such funds go? Bond yields are a less useful market signal when the Fed is manipulating them. And many central bankers get antsy at the thought of zero interest rates for years. They might tempt

hedge funds, banks, and others to "chase yield" by plowing borrowed money into risky investments. A lot of people think the Fed brought on the subprime crisis by keeping rates low from 2002 to 2004. There may be truth to this, but raising interest rates to combat speculation is a bit like using dynamite to eradicate termites: The remedy may do more damage than the problem. A more surgical response is to use regulations to limit risk-taking.

When Monetary Policy Stops Working

Investors and economists have long believed that what a central bank wants, it gets. That belief has been shaken. Japan has had interest rates near zero for more than a decade but its unemployment has never returned to its pre-1990 levels. The United States has had stubbornly high unemployment despite extensive use of unconventional policy.

There are two, competing explanations for why monetary policy may fail to boost spending and employment. One blames supply: The people without jobs don't have the skills that the changed economy needs. Perhaps the economy has languished for so long that their skills have atrophied while business product lines, stores, and factories have turned obsolete. More

monetary medicine will eventually only deliver inflation—as occurred in the 1970s.

The other explanation blames demand. Monetary policy usually works because at some point, interest rates will be low enough to get businesses and households to borrow and savers to spend. But what if potential borrowers don't qualify for loans, or are preoccupied with paying off old debts? What if savers are so pessimistic about the future they would rather earn zero on a bank account than buy a house or invest in stocks? In the 1930s John Maynard Keynes dubbed this a "liquidity trap," in which monetary policy becomes impotent.

Scholars still debate whether a liquidity trap has ever existed, even in the 1930s. Assuming it does, how would you escape it? Leaving aside some technically dubious proposals, deeply negative interest rates are impossible. But negative real rates aren't, and as we learned in Chapter 5, it's the real rate of interest that matters. If inflation is 2 percent and the interest rate is zero, the real interest rate is negative 2 percent. If that doesn't get people to spend, then the Fed could raise its inflation target to 4 percent, or more, and make real rates even more negative.

A related idea is for the Fed to target something else altogether, such as nominal GDP growth, which is simply the sum of real GDP growth and inflation. If the target is 4 percent and real GDP grows only 1 percent, inflation could rise to 3 percent. That higher inflation

would push real interest rates down and eventually boost spending and real GDP.

These ideas have problems, though. Raising inflation is easier said than done; the Bank of Japan has tried, and failed. Since the Fed has worked for so long to keep inflation around 2 percent, the public may not think it's serious about raising it to 3 or 4 percent—assuming the public could figure out what the Fed is up to. Second, stabilizing the public's inflation expectations at 2 percent has paid big dividends: It has made dangerous inflation and deflation both less likely. Consigning such an investment to the rubbish bin should not be done lightly. Finally, it's not clear what tools the Fed would use to get inflation and nominal GDP higher beyond the ones it's already used.

Unconventional monetary policies are like experimental drugs: Researchers have good theories about why they should work, but little practical experience. Side effects might be trivial—or lethal. Doctors prescribe experimental drugs only when the patient doesn't respond to anything else. The Fed feels the same way about unconventional policies.

Raising interest rates to combat speculation
is like using dynamite to eradicate termites.

The Bottom Line

- When setting interest rates, the FOMC weighs how far the economy is from its potential, and how far inflation is likely to be from 2 percent. This is harder than it sounds because the economy responds unpredictably and with lags.

- At FOMC meetings, Fed officials listen and debate the best path for monetary policy. A few dissent but the chairman always carries the day. The Fed gives out so much information that the result is seldom a surprise but it still moves markets.

- The Fed carries out monetary policy by using open-market operations to move the Federal Funds rate, charged on loans between banks, up or down.

- When the Funds rate fell to zero in 2008 the Fed turned to unconventional policies such as quantitative easing: buying up bonds to push down long-term interest rates.

- Monetary policy won't reduce unemployment if it is held up by structural factors, or if a liquidity trap exists.

When the World Needs a Fireman

America's Lender of Last Resort and the World's Crisis Manager

THE COLLAPSE OF THE Twin Towers on September 11, 2001, tore through the infrastructure of Wall Street. Traders' telephones didn't work. The wires over which banks sent payments to each other were severed. A bank that processed half of Wall Street's Treasury bond

trades couldn't confirm what trades had gone through. And the aircraft that shuttled bags of checks between processing centers were grounded. With payments stuck in transit, some banks started to run short on cash while others began to hoard what they had.

Roger Ferguson, the only governor at the Fed that day, issued a statement reminding banks that the Fed was open for business. The following day, banks borrowed $46 billion from the Fed. Where did the Fed get the money? Simple: It printed it. More precisely, it used a few keystrokes and voilà, the money appeared in the banks' accounts at the Fed. When the damage was repaired and the markets returned to normal, the banks repaid the loans and the money disappeared.

Neat trick, huh? This, however, is not some parlor game. In fact, it is the sort of thing for which the Fed was created—to be the financial system's lender of last resort. Most of the time, this role is ignored. The crisis of 2008 brought that role back to the limelight with a vengeance, as the Fed worked its magic by lending to commercial banks, investment banks, an insurance company, money market mutual funds, and others, all to keep financial institutions afloat, maintain the flow of credit to the economy, and thus enable businesses and consumers to keep spending.

───────────── ❧ ─────────────

**Whenever the financial system
catches fire, the phones soon ring at
the Fed station house.**

───────────────────────────────

The Fed's unique power to lend at will makes it the financial system's crisis manager. When fire breaks out in some corner of the financial system, the phones soon ring at the Fed station house in Washington or at the New York Fed in lower Manhattan, whose president talks regularly with the biggest players on Wall Street, foreign central bankers, and finance ministers.

Being crisis manager may not involve lending money; it may mean strong-arming private banks and investors to lend their own money to keep companies or countries from defaulting. The Fed got this role by virtue of its place at the center of world markets and its reputation for nonpartisan professionalism.

The Fed has been called on to play this role with increasing frequency. Although Paul Volcker's defeat of inflation in 1982 ushered in 25 years of tranquil growth, it also led to serial crises.

- In the early 1980s, many big U.S. banks were near-insolvent because of souring loans to Latin

America. Volcker arranged for those loans to be rolled over until the banks were healthy enough to write them off.

- In 1987, the stock market crashed. The Fed cut interest rates and urged banks not to cut off strapped Wall Street brokers.
- In 1994, Mexico devalued the peso and narrowly avoided default with the help of loans from the Fed and Treasury.
- In 1997, when Korea teetered on the edge of default, New York Fed president William McDonough persuaded U.S. banks to renew their loans.
- In 1998, McDonough brokered a rescue of the giant hedge fund Long Term Capital Management.

A Rude Awakening

Like the Fed's apparent success at taming the business cycle, its crisis-management skills may have lulled us into thinking the economy had become a safer, less violent place. As a result, everyone from the biggest banks to the smallest hedge funds came to assume that money would always be easy to borrow. "Money always seems free in manias," noted Charles Kindleberger, a market historian in *Manias, Panics, and Crashes*. That assumption

was shattered on August 9, 2007, when a French bank, BNP Paribas, announced that one of its investment funds, which had sustained big losses on subprime mortgages, would suspend repaying investors their money. The event triggered a global scramble for cash as investors, unsure who'd been left holding the mortgage industry's toxic waste, hoarded their money. Short-term interest rates skyrocketed.

The Fed needed to find a way to inject money into the financial system. It used open-market operations. It lowered the discount rate. It auctioned off loans from the discount window (which I'll explain later in this chapter). In the *New York Times*, Paul Krugman compared Bernanke to television's MacGyver, who "would always get out of difficult situations by assembling clever devices out of household objects and duct tape."

On the evening of March 13, 2008, Bear Stearns informed the Securities and Exchange Commission (SEC), which then told Tim Geithner, then president of the New York Fed, that it, too, was about to run out of cash, and it would have to file for bankruptcy protection the next morning. Unwilling to risk the chaos that would ensue, the Fed the next morning agreed to lend Bear Stearns enough money to stay alive long enough to find a buyer. By law, the Fed ordinarily only lends to

commercial banks, so it had to use a loophole in the law to lend to Bear Stearns, an investment bank. It used the same loophole to lend money to American International Group, an insurance company, to keep it from failing, and it used it to buy asset-backed commercial paper, to lend to money market mutual funds, and to buy the commercial paper issued by companies like General Electric.

The Fed can lend as much as it likes. Need $1 billion? Print $1 billion. By early 2009, it had lent $1.5 trillion. Yet this formidable firepower has a big handicap. A loan from the Fed can help a bank that's temporarily illiquid (i.e., short of cash) as long as it is solvent (its assets are worth more than its liabilities). But Fed lending cannot save a bank that is insolvent. Insolvent banks must be closed or given new capital. New loans simply delay the inevitable. In 2008, rapidly souring mortgage loans meant many U.S. financial institutions were nearly insolvent, or suspected of it, which is why $1.5 trillion didn't stem the panic. The Fed claims it couldn't lend to Lehman Brothers because it was insolvent, though that claim is suspect.

Only when Congress created the Troubled Asset Relief Program (TARP) to invest up to $700 billion to recapitalize banks and buy up bad debt did the panic ease.

———————— ~ ————————

The Fed has a loophole to lend temporarily to companies other than banks, but it sat unused until 2008.

Could the Fed Go Broke?

The Fed doesn't exist to make a profit, but imagine, for a moment, that it does. If we compare it to a regular bank, its balance sheet looks similar. On the asset side it has loans to investment dealers and commercial banks, and securities such as Treasury and mortgage bonds, all of which earn interest. On the liability side, it has reserves, which are essentially commercial bank deposits, on which the Fed usually pays interest. Where the Fed differs from commercial banks is that a huge portion of its liabilities are currency. The Fed, unlike a regular bank, can issue $20 bills, on which it pays no interest, and use it to buy bonds or make loans, on which it earns interest.

This produces a big profit for the Fed, called *seigniorage*, which it hands over to the Treasury. This isn't chump change. In 2006, it paid the Treasury $29 billion. This means every taxpayer has an interest in how the Fed manages its balance sheet.

During and after the financial crisis, the Fed shifted from safe Treasuries to better-paying but riskier things like mortgage-backed securities, loans to banks and AIG, old Bear Stearns assets, commercial paper, and so on. It also vastly increased the size of its balance sheet. As a result, the profit it paid Treasury ballooned to $77 billion in 2011.

This isn't without risk. But the Fed cannot go broke. Its bonds are not carried at market value, so fluctuations in their prices don't matter. Its loans are backed by collateral. Losses on them would have to be ridiculously large to wipe out its profit and capital. Anyway, the Fed doesn't need capital: Unlike a commercial bank, it can never run out of cash to repay depositors since it simply prints what it needs. Of course, asking Congress for more capital wouldn't be good for its independence.

Into the Weeds

Banks are acutely vulnerable to panic. Most of their money is tied up in loans. They keep cash on hand to repay some depositors, but not enough to repay *all* of their depositors.

In 1873 Walter Bagehot, an early editor of the *Economist*, wrote in *Lombard Street*, "A panic grows by what it feeds on. . . . [It is] a species of neuralgia."

In such a panic, investors abandon any kind of risky asset and demand the safest, most liquid thing: cash, or its closest substitute, Treasury bills. Only a central bank can create more cash. Bagehot recommended it lend against any good collateral, at a penalty interest rate to discourage frivolous borrowing.

This is the principle behind the loans the Fed makes from its discount window. (There's no actual window: All this takes place electronically.) It lends to commercial banks, accepting as collateral loans, securities, and other assets discounted from face value. Loans from the Fed to banks are charged the discount rate. To encourage banks to first borrow from each other before borrowing from the Fed, the discount rate is set slightly above the Federal Funds rate target. Over the years, the discount window has dwindled in importance as banks found other sources of funds at home and abroad. Banks used it when the payment system didn't operate properly, as on 9/11, or if they were short of required reserves. Most notoriously, troubled banks used it when no one else would lend to them, as Continental Illinois did in 1984. It eventually failed. This gave the discount window a stigma, and healthy banks avoided it at all costs. Getting around that stigma is why during the recent crisis the Fed made loans from the discount window via auctions: They were cheaper, and more anonymous.

The Federal Reserve Act says the Fed can lend only to banks, thrifts, and credit unions. That made sense when banks financed the economy. But as Chapter 15 will show, they now share that job with mutual funds, investment banks, finance companies, hedge funds, and the like. Instead of deposits, they issue bonds and short-term money market paper or borrow from banks. When the crisis hit, lenders wouldn't refinance their paper or their loans. They faced the equivalent of a nineteenth-century bank run, but with no lender of last resort.

In the 1930s, Congress inserted a loophole in the Federal Reserve Act. Section 13(3) lets it lend to companies other than banks—temporarily. The Fed was reluctant to use 13(3) because such loans favored some borrowers over others and carried a greater risk of loss. And so 13(3) sat largely unused—that is, until 2008.

As the crisis passed, the Fed closed most of its special lending facilities. Having once become lender of last resort to the entire financial system, the Fed may be expected to do so again. Yet Congress, fearing precisely that, put new limits on the Fed's lending authority in the 2010 Dodd-Frank act. The Fed now needs the Treasury secretary's permission to make loans under 13(3), must be sure those loans don't incur losses for the taxpayer, and can't target a loan to a single company,

as it did to Bear Stearns and to AIG. Routine discount window loans used to be confidential; now, the Fed must disclose borrowers' names after two years. Given the stigma of disclosure, some banks may hesitate to use the discount window.

Whether these restrictions interfere with the Fed's ability to do its job, we'll find out in the next crisis.

Lender to the World

Virtually every central bank considers itself a lender of last resort, but how they do their job varies. The Bank of England was founded in 1694 to lend to the crown, whose credit had fallen to subprime status after Charles II stopped paying his bills in 1672. (It became known as the Great Stop of the Exchequer, a euphemism for, "The check is not in the mail.") Almost all modern central banks are lenders of last resort to their commercial banks. In 2011 and 2012, depositors and lenders were yanking money out of banks in the euro-zone, fearing some would go bust or repay them in something other than euros. The European Central Bank responded by lending banks nearly 1 trillion euros for up to three years. Though prohibited from financing a country's deficits, the ECB will play lender of last resort by buying its bonds if a loss of confidence could force it to abandon the euro.

Because of the dollar's importance, the Federal Reserve is sometimes lender of last resort to the entire world. Foreign banks routinely borrow and lend in dollars. If for some reason creditors decide to stop supplying those dollars, where do the banks turn? Foreign central banks can't print dollars. Fortunately, the Fed can help out by printing dollars and then lending them to foreign central banks, which lend the dollars to its own banks. These loans are done under "swap" agreements, which are really just matching lines of credit. For example, the Fed lets the ECB borrow up to $100 billion for 90 days, and the ECB lends the Fed the equivalent in euros. There is no risk to the Fed, except in the unlikely event the ECB defaults. And it helps Americans: If those foreign banks couldn't get dollars they'd have to call in all their dollar loans, driving up interest rates, including for Americans.

The Bottom Line

- The Federal Reserve has made its name managing the economy through monetary policy, but its parents had a different career in mind: to act as lender of last resort when banks ran out of cash. The Fed is uniquely suited to the job because it can simply create whatever money it needs to lend, primarily through loans from

its discount window, and withdraw the money from existence when the loans are repaid.

- During the financial crisis the Fed dusted off a loophole to lend not just to banks but to a wide assortment of companies. In so doing it may have saved the country from another Depression, but it also awakened politicians to its formidable power.

The Elephant in the Economy

~

What the Government Giveth and Taketh Away

IN JULY 1988, Ronald Reagan signed into law the biggest expansion of Medicare since its creation in 1965. Henceforth, the federal health program for the elderly would cover the crippling bills that result from catastrophic illness or injury. Prescription drugs would also be covered. No longer would any senior have to choose "between bankruptcy and death," Mr. Reagan declared.

Senior citizens weren't grateful—they were apoplectic. In Chicago, a group of them screamed "Liar!" "Impeach!" and "Recall!" at one of the most powerful men in Congress. One threw herself on his car, forcing him to flee on foot. The reason they were so unhappy: Unlike most new government programs, the beneficiaries were expected to shoulder all the costs of this one: up to $800 per year. The next year, the law was repealed.

Fifteen years later, George W. Bush did not repeat that mistake. When he signed into law a generous new Medicare prescription drug benefit, the elderly were only asked to cover a slim portion of the cost. The remainder—$14 trillion, by the most comprehensive estimate—would have to be dealt with by future taxpayers.

The government makes its presence felt in the economy in multiple ways, but the most important and controversial is how it spends and taxes, collectively called *fiscal policy*. As the contrasting experiences of Mr. Reagan and Mr. Bush show, Americans have come to love the benefits the federal government delivers. They just hate paying for them.

Fiscal policy arouses strong feelings because it has big effects on the shape of society, effects not everyone agrees with. It provides "public goods": things that benefit everyone but can't be profitably supplied by the private sector, such as national defense, courts, public

health protection, and highways. It provides things society has determined everyone should have regardless of their means, such as education, museums, and parks. And it sends checks to the unlucky, the elderly, the sick, and the poor. All of this is paid for by taxing wages, investment income, profits, retail purchases, and other things, or by borrowing, which means future taxpayers will pick up the tab.

The federal government leaves a big footprint on the economy. From 1970 to 2007, it collected the equivalent of 18 percent of gross domestic product (GDP) in taxes, and spent about 21 percent of GDP. Over the next four years, revenue plummeted to 16 percent while spending leaped to 24 percent, a result of the recession and measures taken to combat it. The difference between those figures results in a budget deficit (more on that in the next chapter). And yet they barely hint at the breadth of things on which the federal government spends, the impact of how it taxes, and the mind-numbingly complex way Congress and the President deal with both.

What the Government Giveth

Federal government spending comes in three types:

1. **Interest paid on the debts taken on since the American Revolution.** For most of the past

decade this type of expenditure was an afterthought, averaging 8 percent of spending and 1.6 percent of GDP. As the national debt climbs in coming years, interest will become a much bigger presence in the budget, consuming some 4 percent of GDP by 2023. There's not much politicians can do about this category.

2. **Discretionary spending**. Anything Congress must authorize anew each year is called discretionary. Most of what the federal government does is discretionary, from national defense (the biggest) to courts, the FBI, medical research, weather forecasts, early childhood education, national parks, and air traffic control. If Congress doesn't pass legislation appropriating funds for discretionary activity, it must stop. For the past decade, about 38 percent of total spending has been discretionary.

3. **Mandatory spending**. Also called *entitlements*, mandatory spending consumes 60 percent of federal spending. Mandatory spending doesn't require an annual appropriation: It's determined by criteria set in law. For example, Social Security benefits are dictated by the terms of the Social Security Act. Congress often amends these laws, but if it does nothing, the spending continues on autopilot.

—————————— ～ ——————————

**Since 1962, the share of federal spending
on defense has traded places with the
share spent on entitlements.**

———————————————————————————

There were no entitlements until the creation of Social Security in 1935. It was joined by Medicare and Medicaid (health care for the poor) in 1965. All have become more generous over time; Social Security now covers spouses, children, and the disabled. Medicare now pays for prescription drugs. In 2010 Barack Obama signed into law the Affordable Care Act, which created a new entitlement: subsidized insurance for workers who participate in state-run exchanges. Like Mr. Reagan in 1988, Mr. Obama paid for his health-care expansion through additional taxes and cuts to Medicare, which is why, like Mr. Reagan's, Mr. Obama's plan was unpopular.

Other, smaller entitlements include welfare, civil service and veterans' pensions, food stamps, and unemployment insurance.

Back in 1962, the federal government spent 9 percent of the nation's GDP on national defense, 3 percent on other discretionary functions, and just 5 percent on entitlements. By 2012, those priorities had

flipped: National defense consumed less than 5 percent of GDP, other discretionary items 4 percent, while entitlements swallowed more than 14 percent. The federal government today resembles a big insurance company with a security sideline.

Entitlements have achieved some remarkable things such as reduced poverty among the aged. But this comes at a rising price. As the population ages, the ranks of retirees will soar. Meanwhile, science continually comes up with new, more expensive ways to treat our ailments. Left unchecked, the bill for Social Security and health entitlements will balloon from 10 percent of GDP in 2012 to 17 percent in 2040, requiring much higher taxes than Americans have ever paid before.

Social Security was originally designed to be financed by payroll taxes. This worked when the taxes paid by workers far outstripped benefits collected by retirees. The extra money went into a trust fund. As the population ages, however, the number of workers per retiree is falling. In 2009, the payroll taxes paid in fell short of benefits paid out for the first time, and over coming years, that deficit will grow.

True, the trust fund still had $2.7 trillion at the end of 2011. But that's economically meaningless: The money consists entirely of federal government IOUs.

Imagine a father who hands his ninth-grade daughter a $100,000 IOU to cover her college tuition. Is college really paid for? Hardly. Four years later, when his daughter goes to college, the father still has to figure out how to raise the money.

The trust fund is similar: an IOU from one member of the government family to another. When Social Security comes to collect, the federal government has to borrow or raise taxes, just as if the trust fund had never existed.

Medicare is partly funded by a payroll tax and by premiums paid by beneficiaries, but these don't cover the program's costs now, and the gap will only grow.

Every year the trustees of Social Security and Medicare report on the gap between future revenue and benefits. Expressed in today's dollars, they put that "unfunded obligation" at $63 trillion, or 4 percent of all future GDP.

What the Government Taketh Away

Spending money is the fun part. Raising the taxes to pay for it is what makes people squeal, and Americans have a long history of squealing. In the 1790s, a tax on whiskey provoked a rebellion against the administration of George Washington. Back then, the government mostly taxed items that were easy to find, such as imports

and liquor. As government has grown, it found other things to tax: wages, investment income, profits, capital gains, gasoline. What hasn't changed is the general surliness that taxes provoke. In 2010, a man angry at the Internal Revenue Service crashed his plane into its office in Austin, Texas, killing an employee.

Let's take a look at where taxes come from. In the past decade individual income taxes have accounted for the largest share, at 44 percent. More than 40 percent of families pay no federal income tax because they earn too little or because of tax breaks (more on them below). However, most workers still pay Social Security and Medicare payroll taxes, as do their employers. These account for 38 percent of federal revenue. Corporate income taxes account for 10 percent. Finally, excise taxes on fuel, cigarettes, liquor, imports, and so on contribute 3 percent of revenue. Everything else, for example, user fees, contributes 5 percent.

In Search of a Better Tax System

In a perfect world, taxes would be efficient and fair. How far from perfection is the American system? Let's look at efficiency first.

All taxes discourage what's being taxed and by default encourage what isn't. An efficient system raises

money while distorting the economy as little as possible (except when taxes are intended to discourage something, like smoking). By this standard, the American tax system is pretty lousy. Relative to other countries, the United States relies more on taxing wages and investment, thereby discouraging both; and less on taxing consumption. Though it has state and local sales taxes, it is the only rich country without a value-added tax. (A VAT is charged at each stage of production: A business pays VAT on its purchases, collects VAT on its sales, and remits the difference.)

Efficiency also takes a beating from countless credits, deductions, and exemptions. These are collectively called *tax expenditures* because they're simply a form of spending disguised as tax policy. What's the difference between giving a drug company $1 million for conducting research and development, and giving it a $1 million credit against its taxes? None.

Tax expenditures pose several problems. First, they distort activity. For example, deductions for mortgage interest and property taxes encourage people to buy a home instead of renting. Second, they're complicated, and a big reason why the tax code is a mess: It runs roughly 3.8 million words (no one is actually sure—it's that complicated) and compliance consumes 6.1 billion hours a year.

Third, they are expensive, worth more than $1 trillion a year in foregone revenue. Every break seems unobjectionable when enacted. Who doesn't want more research and homeownership? But they force everyone to pay higher income tax rates to make up for the lost revenue. As income tax rates rise, they become a bigger disincentive to work and invest.

Indeed, in the 1970s and 1980s, conservatives, like economist Arthur Laffer and Congressman Jack Kemp, claimed that tax rates were so suffocating that tax cuts would actually pay for themselves by stimulating the supply side of the economy: As people worked and invested more, tax revenue would actually go up. The *supply siders* were wrong: Tax revenue fell after Ronald Reagan's and George W. Bush's tax cuts and it rose after Bill Clinton's tax increases.

At the margin tax rates do affect work and investment incentives, but it's hard to detect with so much else going on. In a 2012 study, economists Emmanuel Saez, Joel Slemrod, and Seth Giertz concluded raising rates by 1 percent reduced tax revenue by 0.1 percent to 0.4 percent, by discouraging work and encouraging tax avoidance.

So American taxes aren't very efficient. Whether they are fair is subjective and economics is lousy at subjective questions. Most Republicans and Democrats agree taxes

should be progressive, which means that the rich should pay higher rates than the middle class, and the poor should pay little or no tax. They differ, however, on how progressive, and even on how to measure the concept.

As we learned in Chapter 4, economic trends have made wages more unequal. The tax system traditionally muted some of that inequality because people at the top pay far more of their income in taxes than the middle class. The difference narrowed after Bush cut tax rates in 2001 and lowered taxes on interest and dividends in 2003. He also cut taxes on lower-income families, but because they paid so little to start with, they didn't see their after-tax income rise nearly as much as the wealthy did.

If the budget was balanced, this wouldn't be a big deal; the tax system could continue as it is indefinitely. But the size of the deficit suggests that taxes will have to rise. Liberals would prefer that they rise more on the rich than the rest, because they have benefited so much from economic and tax trends in the past few decades. Conservatives counter that raising rates on the rich would discourage work and investment, without raising enough money to solve the problem unless the middle class paid more, too.

When Glenn Hubbard left his job as a tax adviser in the Treasury in 1993, he scrawled a message to his

successor on the blackboard: "Broaden the base, lower the rates," over and over, then covered it with wax so that it could not be erased. "The government charged me for my bit of vandalism. But it was worth it," he later wrote.

Hubbard, a Columbia University economist, is of a mind with many economists who think the tax system could be made both more efficient and fairer by lowering marginal rates, and broadening the income base on which taxes are paid by closing breaks.

Easier said than done. This sort of tax reform runs into two problems. The first is that the biggest tax breaks, where the real money lies, are quite popular: Want to cut the mortgage interest deduction? Prepare to take on every homeowner, builder, realtor, and banker in the country. Eliminate the break for municipal bond interest? Don't expect mayors and governors to take it lying down.

Then there's the fact that while the wealthy get a lot of tax breaks, in dollar terms most go to the lower and middle class. The earned income tax credit, for example, goes almost entirely to the poor or nearly poor. The tax breaks for mortgage interest, retirement savings, charitable giving, health insurance, and state and local taxes are popular precisely because so many people benefit from them.

~

**The United States' budget is more like
sausage, a mixture of ground meat from
different parts of the animal stuffed
into a misshapen skin.**

Into the Weeds

Reconciling this multitude of competing priorities for
spending and taxes is the job of the federal budget. In
parliamentary systems, like Britain's and Canada's,
the prime minister draws up a budget and Parliament
passes it. It's like a steak: A solid cut of meat that
changes little between the cow and the dinner plate. The
United States' budget is more like sausage, a mixture of
ground meat from different parts of the animal stuffed
into a misshapen skin.

Let's take a look inside the sausage factory. Under
the Constitution, the president can only propose spend-
ing and taxes; Congress has final say, subject to the pres-
ident's veto. In its first century of existence, the United
States had no federal budget. In 1921, the president
began formulating a single budget with the creation of
what is now called the Office of Management and
Budget (OMB).

~

**Even during the best of times, Congress
routinely ignores requests by the president
to kill pet programs or tax breaks.**

Though the fiscal year begins October 1, the budget process begins a year and a half earlier when federal agencies submit their budget requests to the OMB. No later than the first Monday in February, the OMB submits the president's budget to Congress. How much he actually gets depends a lot on his approval rating—Congress grants a popular president more of what he wants—and his party's control of Congress. But even during the best of times, Congress routinely ignores requests by the president to kill pet programs or tax breaks.

After receiving the president's budget, Congress starts its own process. The Senate and House budget committees pass a budget resolution that sets out spending and revenue totals to which all other tax, program, and appropriations bills should conform. The resolution isn't a law, and can't be vetoed by the president. Both chambers are supposed to pass the resolution by April 15, though they routinely miss this target. And at least four times since 1998 Congress couldn't agree on a resolution at all.

After the resolution passes, and even if it doesn't, individual committees get to work. Tax proposals are handled by the Finance Committee in the Senate and the Committee on Ways and Means in the House. Mandatory spending proposals are assigned to the relevant authorizing committee—Medicare to the Finance and Ways and Means committees, food stamps to the agriculture committees, and student loans to the education and labor committees.

Discretionary spending is the purview of the House and Senate appropriations committees. Each has 12 subcommittees whose chairmen are dubbed "cardinals," dealing with a particular part of the budget. This is the favored time for individual lawmakers to earmark money in an agency's budget for a special projects or constituents, such as a bridge to nowhere in Alaska or swine manure research. Earmarks have evolved from a relatively harmless way for legislators to promote their state or district to a vehicle for vote-buying and even corruption. But they are economically insignificant. They seldom exceed 1 percent of federal spending, and only result in the reallocation of money that would be appropriated anyway.

Getting discretionary spending bills into law is essential because the federal government can't spend money that Congress hasn't appropriated. Since Congress routinely misses the October 1 deadline to

pass all 12 of its appropriations bills, it usually has to pass a *continuing resolution* to fund the government in the interim. Some years, Congress and the president deadlock and, with no authority to spend money, the government shuts down, most famously in December, 1995. Emergency functions, such as national defense and air traffic control, can continue, but employees get IOUs instead of paychecks until the deadlock ends.

Multiple appropriations bills are routinely merged into a single *omnibus bill* either to speed things up or to force through provisions that might not pass on their own. If more money is needed after the fiscal year begins, Congress passes a *supplemental bill*.

If individual spending and tax bills don't total up to what the budget resolution envisioned, they are, in theory, forced to conform through a process called *reconciliation*. Reconciliation has since evolved into a vehicle for major legislative changes. Unlike most bills, reconciliation bills cannot be filibustered in the Senate so they can pass with 51 instead of 60 votes, and debate is limited to 20 hours. This makes it attractive for contentious legislation, such as Bush's tax cuts and parts of Obama's health-care overhaul. Reconciliation, however, has its limits—its Byrd rule forbids amendments that are *nongermane*, meaning they have nothing to do with the budget. Provisions that widen the deficit must expire after 10 years.

~

In budget battles, hyperbole and partisan exaggeration are the weapons of choice. Thank goodness for the Congressional Budget Office.

In budget battles, Congressional leaders and presidents regularly indulge in hyperbole and partisan exaggeration. Thank goodness for the Congressional Budget Office (CBO). Though appointed by Congressional leaders, the CBO director is nonpartisan and doesn't endorse bills. By evaluating their impact and cost, though, the director can make or break them.

The CBO gets things wrong, sometimes spectacularly. But its errors are unbiased. They result from misjudgments or mistaken assumptions, not a presumption that a policy is good or bad.

The CBO shares its watchdog role with Congress' Joint Committee on Taxation (JCT). Although its chief of staff is a partisan appointment, the committee's role and its staff are nonpartisan. The JCT analyzes and helps write tax legislation. The CBO uses its revenue estimates to estimate the cost of legislative proposals.

The budget process works when the problems are manageable and the two parties can compromise. It doesn't when they disagree vehemently on the role and

size of government, as has been the case lately. That's why so many tax and spending provisions are temporary, and why politicians keep turning to commissions, triggers, and sequesters (an automatic spending cut) to impose a solution from the outside, usually in vain.

The Bottom Line

- The federal government is a gigantic player in the economy and it will get bigger in coming years as government services expand, the population ages, and interest on the national debt mounts.

- Federal spending comes in three varieties:

 1. Interest on the debt.

 2. Discretionary spending.

 3. Mandatory spending.

- Tax revenue comes mainly from personal and corporate income and payroll taxes. Compared to other countries, the United States relies relatively little on consumption taxes such as on gasoline or a value-added tax.

- Every year the president proposes a budget; Congress accepts some of it but ignores a lot as it passes the appropriations, tax, and mandatory program laws.

Good Debt, Bad Debt

How Government Borrowing Can Save or Destroy an Economy

GEORGE PAPANDREOU RAN FOR election in 2009 promising to reinvigorate Greece's recession-gripped economy by raising public salaries, investing in infrastructure, and helping small business. Shortly after becoming prime minister he discovered the budget deficit had exploded to 13 percent of Greek gross domestic product (GDP), much bigger than the previous government had let on. Investors fled the country's bonds, driving their

interest rates up to punishing levels. Papandreou was soon slashing salaries and raising taxes. It wasn't enough. In 2012, Greece defaulted: Its lenders wrote off more than half of what they were owed.

Government borrowing is like Ritalin. At the right dosage it can jolt a lethargic economy out of recession. Overdosing, as Greece discovered, can bring on seizure.

In recent years the world has seen examples of both. To understand where the United States is headed, it helps to look at where it started.

At its birth, the United States was a fiscal pariah. It was in arrears on loans taken to pay for its war of independence; the Continental Congress had printed money to pay for its debts and paid soldiers with IOUs.

Government borrowing is like Ritalin. At the right dosage it can jolt a lethargic economy out of recession. Overdosing, as Greece discovered, can bring on seizure.

Alexander Hamilton was convinced that a great nation needed sterling credit and so set about restructuring and resuming payments on the national debt.

The republic redeemed its soldiers' IOUs, including any sold to speculators. In a famous compromise with Thomas Jefferson, Hamilton persuaded Congress to assume the colonies' debts in return for moving the capital from Philadelphia to present-day Washington.

For most of the next century and a half, the federal government was small and conservatively run. The budget was in surplus more often than deficit; the national debt in 1860 was lower than in 1791. (A *deficit* occurs when the government's revenue falls short of spending in a particular year. The *debt* is the sum of all deficits ever run.)

All that changed in the 1930s. In five of every six years since, the government has run a deficit and the national debt has steadily risen. Although a family that borrows every year to pay its bills would eventually have its credit cards canceled and file for bankruptcy, countries are different. As long as debt doesn't grow faster than GDP, lenders shouldn't question its ability to repay. In theory the government can tax the entire GDP if necessary to repay the money—something no individual or company can do.

Three's a Crowd

Debt isn't evil: There's nothing wrong with the government borrowing to finance an investment, such as a

highway, that pays off long into the future. The highway increases potential GDP, and thus the capacity to repay debt, so future taxpayers help pay for something that also benefits them.

But debt taken on to finance current consumption is simply a transfer to today's citizens from tomorrow's taxpayers who must pick up the tab, with interest.

All else equal, government borrowing chips away at long-term economic growth. Imagine a watering hole on the African savannah with just enough water to support a pride of lions and a herd of zebras. Then one day, a bunch of elephants move in. Soon, lions and zebras are dying of thirst. The pool of savings from which businesses and households borrow is like that watering hole. When government deficits start drawing on that pool, the three-way competition for money pushes up long-term interest rates and crowds out private investment— perhaps a family decides not to buy a house or a business decides not to expand. That hurts future growth.

A study in 2004 by Peter Orszag and William Gale found a deficit of 3.5 percent of GDP (roughly its average since 1982), year in and year out, raises interest rates and shrinks the economy by 1 to 2 percent.

Note that I said "all else equal." All else is seldom equal. First, as we learned in Chapter 7 the pool of savings nowadays is global. The federal government

doesn't have to borrow from Americans; it can put the touch on Chinese, Saudi, and German savers. Mind you, this isn't costless. Repaying those foreigners drains national income. Their purchases of Treasuries push up the dollar, hurting exports.

Second, the above example only applies when unemployment is at its natural rate. Then, new jobs created by government borrowing come at the expense of existing jobs. This doesn't apply when unemployment is high. Indeed, deficits automatically expand during recessions as people lose hours, bonuses, or jobs and pay less taxes while collecting more in food stamps, welfare, Medicaid, and unemployment insurance. These *automatic stabilizers* funnel additional spending power into the economy. Meanwhile, households and companies turn cautious and borrow less, freeing up savings, so a higher deficit doesn't crowd out private investment.

Third, all these rules change when interest rates are zero. We turn to that next.

Stimulus versus Austerity, the Great Debate

Without lifting a finger, the government softens the impact of recessions via its automatic stabilizers. Often it wants to do more: enact an additional tax cut or spending increase. Such *stimulus* is not that useful. It can take

months, even years, to pass the legislation and then spend the money. Tax cuts may be saved rather than spent. The money may go to the politically connected, rather than where it does the most good.

But the main knock on fiscal stimulus is that it's usually redundant. If the economy is weakening, the Federal Reserve can lower interest rates on an hour's notice, and raise them just as quickly when the need has passed. If fiscal stimulus props up GDP, the Fed may not cut rates as much. Worse, deficits may overstay their welcome, pushing spending past the economy's potential. The Fed, fearing inflation, would raise interest rates to pull it back. For these reasons, the stimulus "multiplier"—how much each dollar of stimulus raises GDP—may be less than one, and perhaps even zero.

All this changes if interest rates fall to zero. Here's why: A worker worried about his job security is perfectly rational to save the money he had planned to spend on a new car. Unfortunately, that may cost auto workers their jobs, leaving them with less income and less savings. As this "paradox of thrift" (as Keynes called it) ripples through the economy, unemployment mounts and the total pool of savings actually shrinks.

Typically, the Fed breaks this cycle by getting interest rates low enough to coax savers out of their shells. But in Chapter 11 we learned that if interest rates hit

zero without stimulating borrowing and spending, monetary policy may be helpless. At that point, fiscal stimulus becomes quite powerful. By putting someone back to work, stimulus raises income and spending, which puts even more people back to work. As total income grows, so does the pool of saving. A study by Lawrence Christiano, Martin Eichenbaum, and Sergio Rebelo found the multiplier on additional government spending when rates are zero is at least 1.5. That's why a hefty fiscal stimulus in 2009, after interest rates had fallen to zero, made good sense. It almost certainly kept the unemployment rate from going even higher, although there's no way to know for sure. Doctors test drugs against placebos; macroeconomists don't get the luxury.

The opposite of stimulus is *austerity*: cutting spending and raising taxes to shrink deficits and tame the debt. In a growing economy, austerity may actually help growth by reducing the demand for savings, bringing down interest rates and the dollar, which "crowds in" private investment and exports. But when interest rates are near zero, austerity really hurts, because the Fed can't soften the sting: The multiplier works in reverse.

For some countries, austerity isn't a choice. If their finances are a mess, lenders may worry that big deficits make default more likely, and jack up interest rates, or stop lending altogether. This is a particular risk for a

country that borrows in a currency it doesn't control, as Greece did.

Debt Traps and Debt Crises

Most of the time, debt does its damage gradually, like termites in the attic. As lenders demand higher interest rates, the deficits slowly suffocate private investment and a growing share of national income goes to paying interest on the debt. Year after year this nibbles away at the economy's foundations. Sometimes, though, it is like a fire that races through the house. Investors suddenly decide not to lend at all. Interest rates skyrocket, the currency collapses, and economic activity implodes. It's like the conversation between two characters in Ernest Hemingway's *The Sun Also Rises*. "How did you go bankrupt?" one asks. "Two ways," the other replies. "Gradually and then suddenly."

∾

Investor confidence is crucial. An otherwise bearable debt becomes intolerable if interest rates rise sharply.

Unfortunately, it is hard to know in advance whether a crisis will be gradual or sudden. A key danger sign is a

high and rising debt-to-GDP ratio. Investor confidence is crucial. An otherwise bearable debt becomes intolerable if investors suddenly demand sharply higher interest rates. A tipping point occurs when interest rates climb above a country's nominal growth rate. At that point, the debt-to-GDP ratio will automatically rise unless the country runs a budget surplus, excluding interest. For example, if a country's nominal GDP grows 4 percent and it pays 6 percent interest on its debt, it needs an annual surplus, excluding interest, of 2 percent of GDP to keep the debt steady as a share of GDP.

Walter Wriston, the legendary chief executive of Citicorp, was ridiculed for saying countries don't go bankrupt, after Latin American loans almost wrecked his bank. But he was right: A creditor can't drag a deadbeat country through bankruptcy court and grab its assets. (At least, not anymore; the United States occupied Haiti in 1915 to ensure its debts were repaid.) Countries may default because they can't pay or because they don't want to. So lenders must worry about a country's ability and willingness to pay.

These differences explain why some countries can go longer without a debt crisis than others. At the end of World War II, the United States' debt reached 120 percent of GDP, and Britain's 200 percent; neither

experienced a crisis. Nor has Japan, even though its debt at the time of this writing exceeds 200 percent of GDP. By contrast, Mexico's debt was only 35 percent of GDP when a crisis struck in 1994.

In general, investors give a longer leash to countries with a long history of paying their debts like the United States, Canada, and Britain. Such countries are often allowed the luxury of borrowing in their own currency, which insulates them from one of the major causes of debt crises: the inability to repay foreign currency debt. They also get to borrow for 5 to 30 years at a time, which avoids another crisis precursor: dependence on short-term debt. A country (or company) can be left in the lurch if creditors decide not to renew the loan. It's like reapplying for your job every three months.

Countries escape debt through one of five ways. The most painless is to grow its way out: Economic growth generates revenue to shrink the deficit and brings down the debt-to-GDP ratio.

Another way of controlling debt is austerity. This is how rich countries like Ireland and Denmark in the 1980s and Canada in the 1990s escaped their debt traps and it is how the United States turned things around in the early 1990s. Another way is a bailout, when another country or the International Monetary Fund (IMF)

comes to the rescue as the United States did for Mexico in 1994—although austerity is often a condition of such rescues.

Then, for countries like the United States that borrow in their own currencies, there's inflation, which reduces the real value of existing debts. However, creating inflation is easier said than done. And it may not help: If investors smell inflation, they'll charge higher interest rates or refuse to lend. The government may have to use what economist Ronald McKinnon labels *financial repression*: twisting the central bank's arm into keeping interest rates low, or forcing private citizens and banks to buy its bonds at artificially low rates.

The fifth route out of a debt trap is to default.

Could It Happen Here?

The United States' deficits are chewing away at the rafters, but are they about to burn the house down? It doesn't seem likely. Hamilton's legacy endures: Investors' faith in U.S. debt is buttressed by history, politics, and law. The only time the United States did anything like defaulting was its decision in 1934 not to honor previous promises to repay in gold. Crises almost never happen to countries that borrow in their own currency, and the dollar isn't just any old currency, it's the world's reserve currency. As we saw in Chapter 1,

the U.S.'s long-term economic outlook is brighter that most countries' thanks to higher population growth.

~

Crises used to be restricted to emerging countries. Not anymore.

But there are reasons to worry. Crises used to be restricted to emerging countries. Not anymore, as Iceland and the euro-zone have shown. At the time of this writing, the debt is 73 percent of GDP and rising, higher than any time since 1950. Back then it owed the debt mostly to its own citizens. Today, the United States owes half to other countries, who may be quicker to flee if they smell trouble. Keeping the confidence of investors doesn't mean balancing the budget tomorrow. It means having a credible plan to stop the debt-to-GDP ratio from heading higher over the next 10 to 20 years. That, however, means painful decisions to raise taxes, slow the growth in entitlements, or both.

Into the Weeds

The Treasury Department's oldest function is to raise the money needed to fund the government by collecting taxes and issuing debt. It has numerous ways of

borrowing, but the most important is through public auctions of Treasury bills and bonds.

Total Treasury borrowing is limited by the debt ceiling, truly one of the silliest laws in international finance. Historically, Congress authorized debt issues one at a time depending on the purpose. Eventually borrowing authority was consolidated into a single debt limit. The result is that Congress can approve a budget that includes a deficit, and then must separately approve the borrowing to fund that deficit. In other countries, the budget and borrowing are a single law. Politicians routinely vote for spending and tax policies that create deficits, and then sanctimoniously inveigh against the higher debt ceiling needed to fund them. They typically hold on for some sort of concession from the president before approving the increase.

In 2011, Republicans' opposition to raising the debt ceiling stiffened considerably; many refused to vote for an increase in any circumstance. Unable to borrow, the federal government would have had to renege on something: social security or Medicare checks, soldiers' salaries, perhaps, even interest on the debt, bringing on default. With just days to spare the two sides struck an uneasy compromise. The prospect of repeated brinkmanship prompted a credit rating agency to lower the United States' credit rating from AAA, meaning it is

no longer in the ranks of the world's most trusted borrowers.

Treasuries are the world's most heavily traded and trusted security and the volume of bids at auctions routinely exceeds the amount for sale by a factor of two to three. For the Treasury to sell less than it needs would be like the Jonas Brothers failing to sell out a high school gym: It would be a shocking blow to U.S. prestige and investor confidence. The Treasury carefully manages the process to avoid that.

So how big is the national debt? Well, it depends on one's definition of national debt of which there are quite a few as Table 14.1 shows. In September 2011, the gross federal debt was almost $15 trillion or 99 percent of GDP. However, almost $5 trillion of this is owed to other parts of the federal government, principally the Social Security and Medicare Trust funds. That debt doesn't trade in the markets. After excluding that debt, the publicly held debt drops to $10 trillion, or 68 percent of GDP. After subtracting federal financial assets, and adding state and local debt, general government debt comes to $12 trillion, or 81 percent of GDP.

The Hidden National Debt

Taxpayers are on the hook for far bigger obligations than just the bonds the Treasury has issued. The

Table 14.1 How Big Is the National Debt?

(As of September 2011)	$ Trillion	Share of GDP (%)
Gross federal debt	14.8	99
Minus debt owed to other parts of the government (e.g., Social Security Trust Fund)	*4.6*	
Equals publicly held debt	10.1	68
Minus federal government financial assets	*1.0*	
Equals net federal debt	9.2*	61
Add state and local debt (excluding receivables)	*3.0*	
Equals general government debt	12.2	81

* Sums may not add due to rounding.

Source: U.S. Treasury; Office of Management and Budget; Federal Reserve.

present value of health and pension benefits promised to future civil service retirees and veterans amount to some $5.8 trillion. Then there's the $63 trillion unfunded liability in Social Security and Medicare.

~

> Unfunded obligations are based on current forecasts and current law. But forecasts can change and Congress can change the law.

These debts, however, are different from Treasury debt: They're estimated obligations based on current

forecasts and current law. But forecasts can change and Congress can change the law, and indeed, it probably will. It may pay a political price but it is not as traumatic as defaulting on a bond.

Finally, Uncle Sam has in effect cosigned trillions of dollars of others' loans with various backups and guarantees. For example, the Federal Deposit Insurance Corporation (FDIC), has guaranteed the safety of $7 trillion in deposits. The Pension Benefit Guaranty Corporation backs private pension plans. Ginnie Mae has guaranteed $1.3 trillion of mortgages insured by the Federal Housing Administration and Veterans Administration. And, most contentious of all, since 2008 the federal government has stood behind more than $5 trillion of debt and guarantees issued by Fannie Mae and Freddie Mac, two formerly privately controlled mortgage companies that became insolvent during the financial crisis.

The actual risk is much smaller than those hair-raising figures imply. Few of those guarantees will have to be honored because most banks won't fail and the costs of those that do will be paid for by the rest. Ginnie Mae, Fannie Mae, and Freddie Mac can repay most of their own debts with the fees, interest, and principal from the mortgages they own or guarantee. But crises

and recessions have a way of turning these contingent liabilities into real ones.

The Bottom Line

- Chronic deficits compete with private borrowers for limited savings driving up interest rates, retarding investment, and impairing future economic growth. Interest on the national debt starves other government programs.

- Budget deficits can be good. During recessions, tax revenues fall and spending on the poor and unemployed rises, softening the sting. There's less competition with private borrowing.

- Governments sometimes use fiscal stimulus—that is, a deliberate increase in the deficit—to boost a weak economy. This is usually unnecessary, unless the Fed is unable to do the job because it has already cut interest rates to zero.

- A breaking point can come when debt is so high that investors suspect governments will try to renege either by defaulting, or through inflation.

- The United States' long history of fiscal probity, favorable long-term growth outlook and control of the world's reserve currency, suggest it has a long way to go before it faces a crisis, but the risk can't be rule out.

Love-Hate Relationship

*The Bipolar Financial System—
Essential for Economic Growth
but Sometimes It Goes Nuts*

In TOM WOLFE'S 1987 novel *Bonfire of the Vanities*, a
bond trader's daughter asks him what he does for a liv-
ing. His wife explains, "Just imagine that a bond is a
slice of cake, and you didn't bake the cake, but every
time you hand somebody a slice of the cake a tiny little
bit comes off, like a little crumb, and you can keep that."

That image pretty much sums up the popular view of financiers: They don't make anything, they just get rich rearranging the fruits of others' labor. At times of crisis, that cynicism turns venomous, such as when Charles Grassley, a Republican senator, in 2009 urged the richly paid employees of one bailed-out firm to resign or commit suicide.

Yet, finance is as essential to economic growth as it is unpopular among Congressmen. The financial system channels capital from those who have it to those who need it, much as the circulatory system moves blood from the heart to the lungs and muscles. A simple example shows how. Imagine that you have money to invest while a colleague at work needs money to buy a house. Why not bypass the bank, and lend him the money? Well, he may need more than you have. He may want to borrow it for 10 years but you only want to lend it for one year. Most important, you don't know if he'll pay it back.

The financial system solves all these problems. It matches savers with borrowers with neither having to know each other. It conducts the necessary due diligence; if the borrower defaults, the saver still gets his money back. It also spares the borrower the burden of repaying the saver before he's done with the money.

The U.S. financial system is one of the most diverse and complex in the world—sometimes too complex for its own good. Thomas Philippon, an economist at New York University, estimates that in 1947, finance accounted for 2.3 percent of GDP. By 2005, it was almost 8 percent. That's an awful lot of cake, and a lot of it was just sugary icing with no nutritional value: leveraged buyouts, speculative stock trading, and financial engineering whose main purpose was to layer on more bets.

But just because finance has its periodic excesses shouldn't blind us to the fact that most of the time it is not just useful but essential. There are no rich countries without banks. History shows that financial innovation usually helps growth; it doesn't hurt it. Something akin to joint stock companies in ancient Rome helped spread large-scale mining technology. Preferred shares were one of the financial innovations that made the railroad-building boom of the nineteenth and twentieth centuries possible. Countless studies also have found that countries with more developed financial systems grow faster.

So does the diversity of the U.S. financial system encourage competition and growth, or does it feed speculation and breed crises? In fact, it does both.

Where Have You Gone, George Bailey?

Think of our financial system in two parts:

1. **Institutions.** This part includes regular banks, investment banks, and *shadow banks* (i.e., companies that act like banks but don't take deposits).
2. **Capital markets.** This part comprises securities and derivatives that investors trade back and forth.

Banks remain the foundation of our financial system, but over the years their importance has shrunk.

Let's look at institutions first. A bank is the most basic part of the financial system, and the most basic sort of bank looks like the Bailey Building and Loan Association run by George Bailey in the film *It's a Wonderful Life*. It starts with shareholder capital, raises deposits, and makes loans.

Banks have gotten a lot more complicated since Jimmy Stewart played George Bailey in 1946. Deposits now contribute just 70 percent of their funding; they get

the rest from bonds, short-term IOUs like commercial paper, wholesale loans from other banks and big investors, derivatives, and other things. They lend to countries, companies, and individuals through loans, securities, credit cards, lines of credit, and countless other avenues.

Although banks remain the foundation of our financial system, their importance has diminished. In 1980, banks supplied 50 percent of the economy's credit; by 2007, that had shrunk to 23 percent. Capital markets, which I'll describe more below, and institutions that look, act, and smell like banks but aren't regulated like banks have taken on a larger lending role. These shadow banks, as PIMCO, the bond fund manager, calls them, match savers and borrowers, but they don't take deposits. Instead of deposits, shadow banks fund their loans by issuing bonds and short-term IOUs or by getting rid of their loans through securitization.

You've probably done business with a shadow bank. Some are neighborhood fixtures, like mortgage brokers, payday lenders, and leasing companies. Others are nationally known. Fannie Mae and Freddie Mac, for example, guarantee or hold mortgages; Ally Financial, the former General Motors Acceptance Corporation (GMAC), makes car loans, and General Electric

Capital Corporation makes leases and loans to businesses. Subprime mortgage lending was dominated by shadow banks like New Century Financial, now bankrupt, and Countrywide Financial, now part of Bank of America.

Money market mutual funds are a type of shadow bank. They purchase commercial paper and other IOUs issued by companies and banks. They fund these purchases by issuing shares to investors. Because funds promise to always redeem shares at a constant dollar each, investors treat their shares almost as deposits. This makes money funds vulnerable to runs, just like banks, though they're not regulated like banks. Investment banks, also called *broker-dealers*, are another type of shadow bank. Rather than lend money directly, they match savers and borrowers in the markets by underwriting and trading stocks, bonds, and other securities; deliver the proceeds to the borrower or company; and take a fee in the process.

———————— ≈ ————————

For all their myriad names and legal charters, banks and shadow banks live or die by two things: capital and liquidity.

Over the years, the lines between banks and shadow banks have blurred. Commercial banks now trade stocks and bonds and investment banks make loans. Loans themselves are often chopped up and turned into securities. Commercial banks provide back-up credit to shadow banks, in effect acting as their lenders of last resort. Commercial banks and shadow banks may be part of the same holding company. Some shadow banks like Ally Financial and General Electric Capital own banks of their own.

For all their myriad names and legal charters, banks and shadow banks live or die by two things: capital and liquidity.

Capital is like armor on a warship. More armor makes a warship more resistant to enemy fire, but slower. With greater capital a bank can endure more loan losses, but it is less profitable because its profit must be spread among more shareholders.

The ratio of assets to capital is called *leverage* and it is an indicator of how reliant a company is on debt. Consider Bank A: It has $1 of shareholders' capital, raises $9 in deposits, and makes $10 in loans. Its leverage is 10. If it gets another dollar of capital it can make $10 more in loans. Bank B, however, has leverage of 20: With each additional dollar of capital it can make $20 in loans. You can see why banks and their shareholders

like leverage. But leverage works in reverse as well. Just as a thinly armored warship is more easily sunk, a thinly capitalized bank is more likely to fail. For Bank A to become insolvent and have its capital wiped out, 10 percent of its loans would have to go bad. For Bank B, just 5 percent would.

Federal regulations previously required banks to hold capital of at least 8 percent of assets, while shadow banks get by with far less. This is one reason why more of them failed during the financial crisis. For example, Fannie Mae and Freddie Mac operated with capital of less than 4 percent to juice their profits. But when mortgages turned sour, their capital disappeared and taxpayers bailed them out.

Liquidity refers to cash and things that are almost like cash that can be used to meet pressing needs. Your house may be worth $300,000, but that's not much help if you need $5,000 today to replace a broken furnace. So you keep cash on hand or a home-equity line of credit for the unexpected. It's the same for a bank. If it can't pay back depositors and lenders, it will fail. So banks keep cash in the vaults, hold securities (like Treasury bills) it can quickly sell, or maintain lines of credit with other lenders. They can also borrow from the Federal Reserve.

If capital is a warship's armor, liquidity is its ammunition. Too little liquidity is as lethal as too little capital.

Without it, a bank would succumb to creditors pulling out their money just as a warship that's out of ammo will succumb to enemy fire.

The importance of liquidity was forgotten in the years leading up to the crisis when a tidal wave of easy money fooled many firms into thinking they could always borrow when they needed. But when panic hit, that assumption proved very wrong.

The financial crisis revealed flaws in the way banks measure capital. They could hold less capital against loans deemed safe, but assumptions about "safe" turned out wrong. Some of their capital consisted of quasi-debt rather than shareholder equity. Because shareholders can't ask for their money back, only equity is truly able to absorb losses and thus protect the bank from insolvency.

So in 2010, regulators from around the world agreed on tough new standards called "Basel III" (the third in a series of such rules, named for the Swiss city where the regulators meet). Banks will have to hold much more pure equity, perhaps even more as the business cycle gets long in the tooth, and yet more if the bank is so big that its failure would collapse the system. All this will make banks less profitable and less valuable and loans more expensive. Hopefully, it will also make bank failures and crises less likely.

Capital Markets

Banks and shadow banks have a vital role to play in supplying credit, especially to small businesses and households. But larger firms can raise capital by issuing stocks, bonds, and other types of securities directly to investors. If you belong to a pension plan, have a life insurance policy, or own a mutual fund, you are helping finance business investment as surely as your savings account makes it possible for your bank to lend.

Debt (also called *credit*) and equity (also called *stocks*) serve different purposes. Debt is temporary with limited upside . . . at best. Debt holders get back their principal plus interest, nothing more. They do, however, get repaid first if the venture goes bad. Equity is a permanent: The company has no obligation to ever repay your investment. Equity brings ownership. Stockholders share in the rewards of success and the losses of failure.

———————————— ∽ ————————————

**Stocks are simple and glamorous.
Credit is complicated and dull. Yet it
matters more to the economy.**

Most companies have one common equity or stock. It trades on a public exchange like the New York Stock Exchange and NASDAQ Stock Market where everyone can see it. A company may, however, have numerous types of debt: short-term, long-term, secured, unsecured, convertible to shares, and so on. A lot of this debt is seldom traded so it is poorly suited to a public exchange. Like rare art, you buy it from, or sell it to, a dealer.

Stocks are simple and glamorous. Cable television tracks minute-by-minute moves in the Dow. Friends share stock tips and magazines celebrate entrepreneurs made rich by their initial public offering. By contrast, debt is complicated and dull, usually relegated to the inner pages of the financial papers. Yet it matters more to the economy. Most companies don't issue stock; they are privately held. Households and governments don't issue stocks at all. At the end of 2011, all the stocks in the United States were worth about $23 trillion. All debt was equal to about $54 trillion, of which households owed $13 trillion; businesses, $12 trillion; financial institutions, $14 trillion; and governments, $13 trillion. This means that an interruption in the supply of credit hurts a lot more parts of the economy than a fall in the stock market.

An important difference between banks and capital markets is that while a bank usually holds a loan

until it matures, securities in the capital markets change hands often, and are valued at whatever price they could fetch in the market today. But there have to be a lot of buyers and sellers willing to trade at that price. Straightforward, popular securities like Treasury bonds and shares of IBM are thus highly liquid. Wall Street's propeller heads have made some securities so complex that in times of panic it became impossible for buyers and sellers to agree on a price. What were once liquid markets became dry as the Gobi Desert.

Two popular types of debt security that played a starring role in the financial crisis are the asset-backed security, or ABS, and the mortgage-backed security, or MBS. An ABS or MBS is almost like a share in a mutual fund: It gives you partial ownership of a pool of mortgages, credit card receivables, auto loans, or other securities. They are structured to pay you interest even if some of the loans in the pool go bad.

Mortgage-backed securities are a great idea that Wall Street, as is its habit, took to excess.

ABS and MBS sound exotic, but they're not. They have been around for decades. Here's how they work. Suppose a small bank has made $100 million in mortgages. It can package them as an MBS and sell it to a pension fund or a foreign central bank. It then takes the proceeds of the sale, and makes $100 million more in mortgages.

Wall Street has a bad habit of taking a good idea to excess, and MBSs were no exception. To appeal to more investors, financiers divided MBS into *tranches* with differing characteristics: some that were safer because they were paid interest first, and some less safe because they took the hit if any mortgages in the pool defaulted. Then they took these MBSs and recombined them into new securities called *collateralized debt obligations*, or CDOs.

Years ago you would put your money in a bank and the bank would grant a mortgage to your neighbor. Now, you:

- Put your money in a pension fund
- Which invests in a hedge fund
- Which buys a collateralized debt obligation
- Which holds a mortgage-backed security
- That a bank put together

- Out of mortgages it acquired from a mortgage broker
- Who made the original loan to your neighbor

Did you get all that? Don't feel bad, neither did some of the world's most sophisticated investors. With so many steps, many investors didn't know much about who they ultimately lent to, and simply outsourced their due diligence to credit rating agencies. Those agencies in turn thought the securities were worth AAA ratings because they badly miscalculated how much home prices would fall and how many of these loans would default.

The Teenage Boys of Finance

Derivatives are one of the most maligned and least understood parts of the financial system. They are the teenage boys of finance—energetic and full of potential but the first to be fingered when someone totals the car.

A derivative is a contract whose value is derived from some other price or security: an interest rate, a currency, a stock index, a commodity. The first derivatives were on agricultural commodities. A farmer would enter into a binding contract with a food processor to sell his corn to that same processor six months later, locking in the value of future sales. Now, a U.S. company that

plans to deliver parts to a European customer may use a derivative to lock in today the value of the euros he'll receive in six months' time. Suppose you want a 10-year loan but your bank would rather make a one-year loan. It can make you the 10-year loan, then use an interest-rate swap to make it resemble a one-year loan.

Currency and interest rate swaps are the clean-cut honor roll students of derivatives who almost never cause problems. Credit default swaps (CDSs) are the tattooed skateboarders forever giving the school principal heart palpitations.

The idea of a CDS seems innocent enough. Suppose you made a $100 loan to your brother, but you worry he won't repay you. You pay a bank $5 a year on the condition that if your brother defaults, the bank pays you $100. CDSs thus make it possible for you to hedge your loan. The problem is they also give you less reason to be careful about lending to your brother. CDSs thus may be one reason so many bad loans were made.

Asset-backed securities and derivatives are too useful to disappear. Crises are extremely effective at killing stupid financial innovations.

The growth in derivatives has been nothing short of phenomenal. Between 1998 and 2011, the notional value of derivatives traded over the counter (which means dealer-to-dealer, not on public exchanges) grew eight times to $648 trillion. Now, what's notional value? Suppose you enter a contract to pay 5 percent interest on someone else's $100 loan. The contract's notional value is $100 but your actual exposure is only $5 per year. In this instance, notional value overstates the actual risk.

Nonetheless, this growth has brought dangers. Derivatives encourage leverage because they require less of a down payment than the same bet made with cash. They are also opaque: A company knows how much it owes to a bank or bondholders, but it may not know how many CDSs are riding on its solvency. Orange County, Barings Bank, and American International Group lead a list of organizations that blew their brains out on derivatives. Consequently, derivatives have been prime suspects in many market blow-ups. Portfolio insurance, a popular hedging technique using stock index derivatives, helped cause the 1987 stock market crash.

Regardless of these dangers, ABSs, MBSs, and derivatives are too useful to disappear. Crises kill off stupid financial innovations—the 1987 stock market

crash deep-sixed portfolio insurance and the latest crisis has done the same for exotic mortgage securities. But, derivatives are here to stay. Like teenage boys, though, their potential is best realized with plenty of adult supervision. That means that they require plenty of capital and liquidity and, wherever possible, transparency in the open market, such as on a public exchange instead of in a private dealing room.

A Species of Neuralgia

For all the wonders that finance does for growth, it comes with one big unpleasant side effect: crises. As Carmen Reinhart and Kenneth Rogoff note in *This Time is Different: Eight Centuries of Financial Folly*, crises have been a fixture of finance since 1340 when Edward III of England defaulted, bankrupting the Florentine bankers who financed his war with France. Almost continuously since 1800, some part of the world has been in a banking or debt crisis.

One purpose of the 2010 Dodd-Frank act was to stamp out crises. It created the Financial Stability Oversight Council, described in Chapter 9, which can rein in or even break up any firm it considers a menace to society. The act also provides a way to deal with a teetering company other than the unappetizing extremes of bankruptcy (as with Lehman), or bailout (as with

AIG). Instead, regulators can seize the company, pay off creditors, wipe out shareholders, then liquidate, restructure, or sell the remainder.

In 2011 Barack Obama declared that Dodd-Frank would "prevent the kind of excessive risk-taking that led to the financial crisis from ever happening again." Oh really? The only thing more inevitable than crises is our inability to anticipate them. People, businesses, and investors adapt, so the next threat to the economy may be utterly different from the last. What if the next crisis comes from the government itself?

What won't change are humans' inbred tendency to extrapolate the past, their inability to predict the future, and their regular swings between greed and fear. Shortly after the Federal Reserve was created in 1913, John S. Williams, the Comptroller of the Currency, wrote, "Financial and commercial crises or 'panics' . . . with their attendant misfortunes and prostrations, seem to be mathematically impossible." It wasn't true then. It's not true now.

The Bottom Line

- You don't have to hug your banker, but what he does is essential to economic growth. Banks and capital markets match savers with those who need capital.

- Over the years, banks have been joined by shadow banks that, like banks, made loans but don't take deposits and aren't as tightly regulated. All these institutions need capital to protect against losses and liquidity to repay lenders. Too much of either, and profits suffer. Too little, and the institution could fail.

- Equities get all the attention in the capital markets but the economy relies more on a healthy market for debt securities, such as money market paper, bonds, and asset-backed securities.

- Crises are an inevitable by-product of finance, and pretty much impossible to predict.

Acknowledgments

~

THIS BOOK REFLECTS A lifetime of learning from people too numerous to list. I got my first lessons in economics as a child from my mother, Irene Ip, a practicing economist for many years, now retired. Great editors have taught me to turn the things I discovered about the economy into stories. They include Michael Babad of the *Financial Post* and the *Globe and Mail*, Larry Ingrassia of the *Wall Street Journal* (and now the *New York Times*), and in particular David Wessel, my mentor for 11 years at the *Wall Street Journal*.

There is no more stimulating and rewarding place to write about economics than the *Economist*. I thank John Micklethwait, the editor, for his encouragement on this book and the opportunity each week to write for the

world's most demanding readers; Zanny Minton-Beddoes, our economics editor, for accommodating my schedule and for her extensive and valuable suggestions on the text; Rachel Horwood for her incomparable research assistance; and Jon Fasman for his collegial advice on the trials of writing a book.

Many people lent their time and expertise to help me get various sections of the book right. They include Douglas Irwin at Dartmouth College, Jim Horney at the Center on Budget and Policy Priorities, Tom Gallagher, Stephen Jen of SLJ Macro Partners and in particular Ray Stone of Stone & McCarthy Research Associates. Any errors are my responsibility.

Howard Yoon, my agent, transformed my early concept into a marketable book. At John Wiley & Sons, Debra Englander helped guide the project. Kelly O'Connor's intensive editing under impossible deadlines vastly improved the organization of the book and made it much more readable.

My wonderful children Natalie and Daniel put up with my mental and physical absences. Most of all I thank my wife, Nancy Nantais, who encouraged me to write this book, supported me throughout the long months and late nights it took to finish it, and gave me constant and helpful feedback to the end.

About the Author

GREG IP IS THE U.S. economics editor for the *Economist* magazine, based in Washington, DC. His career spans two decades of financial and economic journalism, including 11 years at the *Wall Street Journal* in both New York and Washington and before that stints at the *Financial Post* and the *Globe and Mail* in Canada. He appears frequently on television and radio, including National Public Radio, PBS, and MSNBC and is a regular on-air contributor to CNBC. He has won or shared in several prizes for reporting. Greg graduated from Carleton University in Ottawa, Canada, with a degree in economics and journalism. He lives in Bethesda, Maryland.